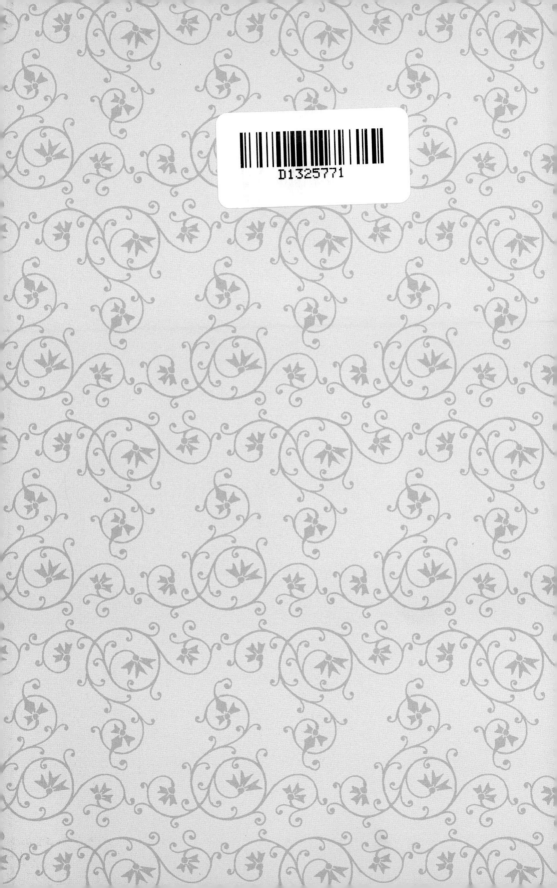

THE
WHITE ROSE
OF GASK

Carolina Oliphant, Lady Nairne, by an unknown artist.

The White Rose *of* Gask

THE LIFE AND SONGS OF CAROLINA OLIPHANT LADY NAIRNE

FREELAND BARBOUR

BIRLINN

First published in 2019 by
Birlinn Ltd
West Newington House
10 Newington Road
Edinburgh
EH9 1QS

All song excerpts are taken from *The Lays of Strathearn*
(Bonskeid Music, 2019)

British Library Cataloguing in Publication Data. A catalogue
record for this book is available from the British Library.

ISBN: 978 1 78027 611 3

Printed and bound by
Gutenberg Press Ltd, Malta

CONTENTS

ACKNOWLEDGEMENTS

I WOULD like to express warm thanks to the following, all of whom have been of great help and support in different ways towards the preparation of this book. They are Jim Hutcheson, Tom Johnstone, Lucy Mertekis and Liz Short of Birlinn; Laurence, Charlie and Gill Blair Oliphant of Ardblair; Donald Smith of The Scottish Storytelling Centre; Bronwen Brown and the staff of the Edinburgh Central Music Library; Cailean Maclean; Margaret Barbour; Caroline Haviland; Amelia Murray Lindsay; Andrew and Seonag Barbour.

PREFACE

SONGS BY Carolina Oliphant, Lady Nairne, are still sung today. Some of them had become hugely popular throughout Great Britain and North America during the second half of her life in the first forty-five years of the nineteenth century, but her name as author was kept well-hidden as a result of her own inclinations and instructions. Partly in consequence of this she has never been accorded the same limelight so rightly enjoyed by Robert Burns both during his own lifetime and thereafter. Unlike Burns she did not die young and she came from a relatively privileged background, nor did she write such a range of works of genius as Burns, but she is without doubt second only to him in that period as a writer of Scots song. The details of her life have never been particularly well-known and the last biography of her appeared in 1900. So when in 2016 The Scottish Storytelling Centre in Edinburgh held a small event to look at her life and songs and mark the 250th anniversary of her birth it seemed that the time was perhaps right to give her another 'crack of the whip' and bring together in a modern context as much material about her life and personality as possible. The 'Flower of Strathearn', as she was known, reached the Land o' the Leal almost a hundred and seventy-five years ago, but her songs live on and her character and personality within them, and long may they continue to do so.

FREELAND BARBOUR
Edinburgh, February 2019.

I
'Gask and Strowan Arena' Slack'

'In 1766 was born the chief ornament of the Gask line. Her birth is set down in a list of births and deaths, reaching from 1668 to 1774, in her father's hand, 'Carolina, after the King, at Gask, Aug. 16th 1766.'*

AND THUS Carolina Oliphant, later to become and be better known as Lady or Baroness Nairne and author of some of Scotland's best-loved songs, made her first appearance in the world. And what a world to arrive in. Only twenty-one years earlier Scotland and to a much lesser extent England had been engulfed in a civil upheaval of immediate consequence to those who found themselves on the losing side, and far-reaching impact for those who lived north of the Highland Line that very roughly divides the mountainous north from the flatter regions of central Scotland. And indeed the young Carolina's own family had experienced exile and loss of home and lands as a direct result of their long and staunch faithfulness to what transpired to be a doomed cause. You would imagine that a happy and peaceful childhood would not be a likely outcome for children born at that time and in such circumstances, but in fact, for the Oliphants, the opposite turned out to be the case.

The old house and lands of Gask lay in Strathearn in Perthshire, on the north side of the River Earn some nine miles west of Perth, and the Oliphant family could trace their ownership from the early part of the fourteenth century. The family of De Olifard, as they were previously known, were Norman in origin and had come to England in 1066 with William the Conqueror. They had fared well as a result, being given land by the King at Lilford in Northampton-shire. There they established themselves until the uncertainties and civil wars between the followers of Matilda (Queen Maud) and King

*From *The Jacobite Lairds of Gask* by T.L. Kington-Oliphant.

Stephen (Stephen of Blois) that followed the death of Henry I and brought anarchy to England between 1135 and 1154. The de Olifards initially took the side of Stephen, but in 1141 David de Olifard saved the life of King David I of Scotland, who was an uncle of Matilda's and had brought an army south in her support, at the siege of Winchester Castle.*

The Scottish King had through marriage held the Earldoms of Northampton and Huntingdon and had stood godfather to David de Olifard while visiting his earldoms on a previous occasion. Why the De Olifards then took the side of Stephen is not clear, but after David, who was then aged barely twenty, had saved his godfather's life, he decided to switch allegiance and accompany King David back to Scotland. In thanks he was given lands including Crailing and Smailholm in Roxburghshire, and later a knighthood as well, and before long was taking a leading role in the life of his new home. About this time the French preposition in the Olifard name appears to have been dropped and young Sir David Olifard was appointed by King David's grandson and successor Malcolm IV as the first Justiciar of Lothian. This post involved the administration of royal justice for the province of Lothian which at that time consisted of all of Scotland south of the Rivers Forth and Clyde and including Northumbria and Cumbria, with the exception of Galloway. It placed the holder to all intents and purposes second only to the King in that area in terms of power and influence. Sir David's son Walter also held this post from about 1178 to 1188. In 1173 Walter had married Christian, daughter of Ferchar, Earl of Strathearn, and received the lands of Strageath (modern day Blackford) near Crieff as dowry. He moved the family to Perthshire, and clearly their

---

*In the words of the chronicle of John of Hexham 'The King of Scotland having lost all his men barely escaped, and made a precipitate retreat to his own kingdom; for a certain godson of his, David Holifard, a comrade of those who besieged the city of Winchester, secreted him, so that those who were in eager search of the King did not discover him.'

prosperity and influence did not diminish over the succeeding century. In 1183 Walter entered into an excambion agreement with his brother-in-law Gilbert, 2nd Earl of Strathearn, and exchanged Strageath for the estate of Aberdalgie and Gask. His son, also named Walter, was also to hold the post of Justiciar of Lothian from 1215 until his death in 1242.

By the end of the thirteenth century we find the name changing to Oliphaunt and in 1296 Sir William Oliphaunt fought under John Balliol in the defeat by Edward I of England at the Battle of Dunbar. Later in 1304 he was second-in-command under his cousin of the same name in holding Stirling Castle against Edward. He also was one of the forty Scottish patriots who in 1320 set their signatures to the Declaration of Arbroath, this being a document sent to Pope John XXII at Avignon which amounted to an appeal for papal support in establishing Scottish independence from Edward II of England. Previously, in 1314, Sir William's son Walter had married Elizabeth, daughter of Robert the Bruce, and after Bruce's victory over the English army at Bannockburn, the Oliphaunt lands of Gask and Aberdalgie were elevated to a barony and this was confirmed by David II in a much-prized Charter of 1364. David II was succeeded by Robert II in 1371 and with him began the rule of the House of Stewart, or Stuart as it became with the accession of James VI in 1567.

Suffice it to say that from 1371, with various rises and falls in fortune, the Oliphant family as they were now known would adhere to this royal house and no other. The family remained at Aberdalgie until the middle of the fifteenth century when they built the nearby castle of Dupplin and were enobled by James II in 1458. In 1513 Colin, the Master of Oliphant and son of the Lord Oliphant of the day, and his brother Laurence, Abbot of Inchaffray, fought and died in the cataclysmic Scottish defeat of Flodden.

Colin left two sons and from the eldest descended the title. The fourth Lord Oliphant fought for Mary Queen of Scots at Langside in 1568 but his son, rather surprisingly for an Oliphant, was implicated in the Gowrie Conspiracy of 1600. This was an attempt by John Ruthven, 3rd Earl of Gowrie, to kidnap James VI at Gowrie House near Perth, and seems to have been to all intents and purposes an attempted *coup d'état*. It failed and led to the fall of the Ruthven family. Young Oliphant was implicated and was fortunate only to be exiled, and the title passed to the fourth Lord's second son, 'ane base and unworthy man' as the Oliphant family papers have it. He died childless, but before doing so managed to bankrupt the estates which by now included land in Perthshire, Caithness, Fife, Forfar, East Lothian and Kincardine.

From Colin Oliphant's second son descended the Oliphants of Gask and the third of this line was able to buy much of the Perthshire lands from his spendthrift cousin. This included a charter, under the Great Seal,* of the lands and barony of Gask, in 1625.

His son Laurence Oliphant was knighted by Charles II at Perth in 1651 and thereafter there was no wavering in the staunchness of Oliphant support for the House of Stuart. The knighted Laurence however possessed a stubborn streak and disinherited his first-born Patrick for his son's refusal to marry a bride of his father's choice.** The estates were passed to the second son Laurence, but his sons George (the third Laird) and William (the fourth Laird) had no children and Patrick's son James inherited Gask in 1705 and became the fifth Laird. He wisely remained at home during the Jacobite Rising ten years later. He had married Janet Murray of Woodend in 1689 and they had

---

*The Great Seal of Scotland replaced the monarch's individual signature and carried the full weight of Royal Decree.

**Patrick was at this time twenty-one years old and the intended bride was Mary, sister of the first Marquis of Douglas. She was a widow and at least forty-five and Patrick's father had set up the match as an aid to an interminable lawsuit that he was involved in. Patrick had never met the lady and retaliated by marrying Margaret, daughter of John Murray, minister of Gask and Kinkell and illegitimate son of the second Earl of Tullibardine.

THE WHITE ROSE OF GASK

fifteen children, their second child being their first son Laurence who became the sixth Laird, and their fifteenth child Ebenezer who was to make his name as a gold and silversmith in Edinburgh.

The seventeenth century was a time of enormous religious upheaval in both Scotland and England. The two kingdoms had been united under the protestant Scottish Stuart King James VI and I but the autocratic ways of his son Charles I led to civil war involving both kingdoms, the success of the Protestant Parliamentarians, the beheading of the King, and the rise to power of Oliver Cromwell. Cromwell's Protectorate came effectively to an end with his death and was followed in 1660 by the restoration of Charles I's son Charles II who like his father and grandfather was a Protestant. But when Charles II died in 1685 he was succeeded by his brother James who had converted to Roman Catholicism in about 1669. James had two daughters by his first wife, the Protestant Anne Hyde, but matters were to come to a head when his second wife, the Catholic Mary of Modena, produced a son and heir in 1688. Sons took precedence over daughters in the line of Royal succession and, given that the new heir would certainly be brought up as a Catholic, the prospect of Catholic succession combined with autocratic behaviour by the king encouraged a group of English noblemen to invite James's son-in-law, the Protestant William of Orange who was married to James's eldest daughter Mary, to bring his army to England and take the Crown.*

Mary and her sister Anne were both Protestant but this 'Glorious Revolution' as it became known resulted in uprisings in both

---

*William and Mary were confirmed as joint rulers of England and Ireland. James VII and II and William were both asked to make presentations to the presbyterian-dominated Scottish Convention in Edinburgh in order to decide who should become king of Scotland, and William was successful here as well. It is an irony of later times that Carolina's grandmother Amelia was in fact descended from the House of Orange through her great grandmother Charlotte de la Tremouille, Countess of Derby, who was the grand-daughter of William the Silent.

William III and Mary II (wax figures in Westminster Abbey).

Scotland and Ireland. The supporters of James became known as Jacobites (from 'Jacobus', the Latin for James) but their military efforts were to prove unsuccessful. In Scotland, though victorious at the Battle of Killiecrankie in 1689, their rising was to peter out shortly afterwards at Dunkeld. In Ireland a more sustained war took place but William and his Protestant forces won overwhelming victories at the battles of the Boyne (1690) and Aughrim (1691) and this for a time brought Jacobite and Catholic resistance to an end.

Never slow to bear arms in the cause of the Stuarts, there had been Oliphants in the Jacobite army at Killiecrankie in 1689, and they were fierce opponents of the deeply contentious and unpopular Act of Union that combined the English and Scottish Parliaments in 1707.*

The reign of William and Mary had been succeeded by that of Mary's sister Anne, but she was to die in 1714. None of Anne's children were to outlive her, despite her seventeen pregnancies, so the Crown was offered to her nearest Protestant relative, George the Elector of Hanover, her second cousin and great-grandson of James VI. He was a German, who incidentally could speak no English, and almost immediately there followed further uprisings in Scotland

*The following verses from Mylne's Manuscript well indicate the strong and wide resentment to the Union felt throughout Scotland at the time:

From forced and divided Union
And from the Church and Kirk Communion
Where lordly Prelates have dominion
Libera nos, Domine. [Free us, O Lord.]

From a new transubstantiation
Of the old Scots into ane English nation
And from all foes to Reformation
Libera nos, Domine.

From paying as our Darien costs
By laying on cess and new imports
From the English ruling Scots rosts
Libera nos, Domine.

From innocent men laying snares
And killing Glenco men by pairs
From sudden death, like the Earl of Stair's
Libera nos, Domine.

James Francis Edward Stuart, 1688-1766, the Old Pretender, by Francesco Trevisani, 1720.

in an effort to annul the Union and put the Stuarts back on the throne.

The first of these in 1715 under the Earl of Mar might well have had more success after the inconclusive Battle of Sherriffmuir near Stirling had it not been for the military indecision of its leader, but

English Jacobites with Scottish support had been defeated a few days earlier by government forces at Preston. Laurence Oliphant, who later became the 6th Laird of Gask and the grandfather of Lady Nairne, was amongst a number of the family name who joined Mar's uprising and was present at Sherriffmuir where he held a commission (Lieutenant-Colonel) in the regiment of his neighbour Lord Rollo. James VII and II had died in 1701 but his son James Stuart, the claimant to the throne and variously styled James VIII and III by the Jacobites or 'The Old Pretender' by his adversaries, arrived in Scotland after Sherriffmuir but after a brief sojourn returned to France in February 1716, abandoning his supporters to fend for themselves.

Laurence was forced into hiding but his father James, the fifth Laird, had not actively joined the Rising and had entailed his lands in favour of his wife and third son James. Thus the house and lands of Gask were not 'attainted' (forfeited) to the London government and remained within the family ownership. Though there were executions and imprisonments following the collapse of the Rising the retribution for the rebels did not last as long as one might have expected and with the Indemnity Act of 1717 it was possible for Laurence, the sixth Laird as he would become on his father's death in 1732, to live openly and marry Amelia, the daughter of William Murray, second Lord Nairne, a Murray from Atholl, and the staunchest of Jacobites. Lord Nairne had command of one of the four regiments of Atholl men in 1715, had been captured at the Battle of Preston and thereafter imprisoned in the Tower of London.

In 1716, after the Rising, he along with his son John had been condemned to death, but had been reprieved at less than two hours notice – not before he had composed his final speech to be delivered from the gallows:

> I forgive all mankind . . . I hope God will support me
> as he did my grandfather the Earl of Derby, who fell a

Laurence Oliphant, 1691-1767, 6th Laird of Gask.

sacrifice for the same cause. God had blessed me with a most tender wife, who is much dearer to me by her virtues than by the Estate she brought me. I commend to God my dear children who have been so dutifull to me. And all my noble and kind Friends who have with so much warmth appeared for me at this juncture, I pray God for them and return them my hearty thanks. – NAIRNE.*

Lord Nairne appears to have owed his last-minute reprieve to James Stanhope, 1st Lord Stanhope, George I's foreign minister and later to become chief minister, on the grounds that they had been schoolboys at Eton together. Nairne's grandfather, James Stanley,

*Excerpts from the scaffold speech of William Murray, 2nd Lord Nairne.

7th Earl of Derby, was a staunch Royalist who had been executed at Bolton in October 1651 at the end of the English Civil War (or War of the Three Kingdoms as it has come to be known). Stanley's daughter Amelia had married John Murray, 1st Marquess of Atholl, and Nairne was the fourth of their twelve children.

The accession of George I consolidated the beginnings of a two-party political system, the ascendancy of Whig interests in London government and with it the decline of the Tory faction, and there is no doubt that this played a part in the Jacobite Risings. The Whigs* were essentially Parliamentarians, constitutional monarchists and, though Protestant, inclined to secular interests as opposed to the Tory party of the day which tended to represent a feudal landed elite in favour of the Royal interest and the attendant influence of the established English Church. Though they didn't know it at the time but may well have sensed it, the Tories were about to embark on fifty years when they had little influence in terms of political power. In Scotland were added the complications of the mainly Catholic Highlands with its paternal clan system and the Protestant Lowlands where the Highlander had long been regarded as a figure of fear.

On the domestic front the period between 1716 and 1745 was not without its vicissitudes for the Gask family. These included an unsuccessful blackmail demand from a Duncan Campbell at Killin who claimed to have been for some time preventing Highland depredations on the Gask lands and stock and was to all intents and purposes

---

*Whig stems from Whiggamore, being the name given to those from the south-west of Scotland who came to Edinburgh annually in order to purchase provisions and in particular grain in the seventeenth century. 'Whig' means to drive and 'more' is a corruption of mare (female horse), so 'Whiggamores' are the drivers of horses or packhorses. The name started to come into general use after the Whiggamore Raid of 1648 when rebel Covenanters from the south-west of Scotland marched on Edinburgh, drove out the Royalist party, and installed the Marquess of Argyll in the seat of power.

Charles Edward Stuart, 'Bonnie Prince Charlie' (1720-88), by Allan Ramsay, c.1745.

looking for protection money, a demand in which he was eventually unsuccessful. There was also a separate dispute with the clan chief, the eighth Lord Oliphant, concerning the sale of family lands in Banffshire from which the clan chief does not emerge with much credit. And all the while the possibility of yet another attempt at the throne for the House of Stuart was never far away. This came to a head in July 1745 with the arrival on the Isle of Eriskay of the Old Pretender's eldest son, Prince Charles Edward Stuart, 'Bonnie Prince Charlie' or 'The Young Pretender' as he was later variously known. Britain was at this time engaged in the War of the Austrian Succession and most of its regular troops were on the Continent. The French King Louis XV had been encouraged by success at the Battle of Fontenoy in May 1745 and had agreed to help Charles with French support, but this consisted of only two ships, *Elizabeth* and the much smaller *Du Teillay*, and a few hundred volunteer troops from the French Irish Brigade. These two ships were intercepted by the British warship HMS *Lion* and in a four-hour engagement *Lion* and *Elizabeth* were both badly damaged and forced to return to their respective ports. Unfortunately for Charles almost all his troops were on *Elizabeth* but he continued and landed in Scotland with a mere seven followers.

From Eriskay they travelled to Glenfinnan where the Jacobite Standard was unfurled in open rebellion. The Highland clans were raised in support and once again Perthshire gentry were not slow to answer the call. The sixth Laird of Gask had by now a family of his own and his son Laurence, Lady Nairne's father and at this time twenty-one years of age, rode north to Blair Castle at Blair Atholl on 1 September where, in his own words:

> I went up with Lord Nairne* to Blair in Athol, where the Prince was with the Hiland army consisting about that time of two thousand five hundred men. I had the Honour to kiss his Royal Highness' hand, kneeling on one knee, and soopt with him afterwards.

Young Laurence was present at the Battle of Prestonpans on 21 September and was able to carry news of the Jacobite victory

*John, 3rd Lord Nairne, grandfather of Carolina's husband William.
He fought with the Jacobite forces in 1715, 1719, and 1745.

back to Edinburgh, despite the attentions of some of General Cope's Government dragoons. From there onwards he acted as an ADC to Prince Charles for the remainder of the campaign. During the march south to Derby his father remained in Scotland as Governor of Perth but rejoined the Jacobite army as it returned north, and both father and son were present at the final defeat at Culloden. Thereafter they managed to escape and go into hiding in Angus and Buchan before fleeing to Amsterdam, from there to Sweden and then later back to France, not to return to Scotland for seventeen years.

The privations suffered by young Laurence during the campaign and his time in hiding resulted in ill-health, particularly asthma, and this was to remain with him for the rest of his life, but he was more fortunate than many of lesser rank who gave the ultimate sacrifice for a cause that may not have meant as much to them as it did to their leaders.

Indeed there seems to have been a general reluctance amongst the tenantry in southern Perthshire to go to war at all and the Laird of Gask, surprisingly given his local popularity, faced more resistance than most. So incensed was he and such was the feudal power enjoyed by landowners of the time that he placed an inhibition or arrestment on his tenants' cornfields, forbidding them to either cut their grain or allow their animals to feed on it, this to be until they should relent and take up arms. This embargo was apparently broken by Prince Charles himself who, in riding with the army from Perth to Stirling, enquired as to why the ripe corn around Gask, where he had just breakfasted, remained uncut. On hearing the reason he is reported to have exclaimed 'This will never do' and, dismounting, he gathered some of the corn, fed his horse, and announced that on his authority the inhibition was now broken. Whether this resulted in a sudden flow of recruits to the Jacobite Standard is not reported.

The Jacobite propaganda at the time of this Gask arrestment in 1745 was beginning to gather momentum and the poets and

The auld house the auld house
What tho' the rooms were wee
Kind hearts were dwelling there,
An' fairies fu' o' glee.

THE AULD HOUSE O' GASK

The birth place of Lady Nairne.

The auld house, the auld house
Deserted tho' ye be,
There ne'er can be a new house
Will seem sae fair to me.

The Auld Hoose o' Gask.

songwriters were busy. Given what was to emanate from the house of Gask a few decades later it's perhaps worth quoting one of the popular ballads of the time which illustrates influences that would later come to fruition:

> Wha' will ride wi' gallant Murray?*
> Wha will ride wi' Geordie's sel'?
> He's the flow'r of a' Glenisla,
> And the darlin' o' Dunkel'.
> See the white rose in his bonnet!
> See his banner o'er the Tay!
> His gude sword he now has drawn it,
> And has flung the sheath away.

*'Gallant Murray' refers to Lord George Murray, sixth son of the first Duke of Atholl and Commander of the Jacobite army and, along with Montrose and Claverhouse in previous campaigns, the most able commander of Highlanders. Murray escaped after Culloden and died in Holland in 1760.

Every faithful Murray follows;
First of heroes! best of men!
Every true and trusty Stewart
Blithely leaves his native glen.
Menzies he's our friend and brother;
Gask and Strowan arena' slack.
Noble Perth has ta'en the field, and
A' the Drummonds at his back.

Sadly for the rebels these exhortations were to prove in vain and after the defeat at Culloden on 16 April 1746 there was a brief re-grouping of the Jacobite leaders and their men at Ruthven Barracks in Badenoch at which both the Oliphants were present. Lord George Murray was for continuing the campaign but his Prince had lost heart and even sent Murray a letter dismissing him from his service. This petulant and graceless act resulted in Murray unleashing a pent-up diatribe against the Prince's ingratitude and incompetence, but by now the campaign was over and the Jacobite army scattered in an effort to save themselves as best they could.

The ravages of the Hanoverian army of the Duke of Cumber-land (third son of George II) throughout the Highlands after Cullo-den have been well-documented. Suffice it to say that any Jacobite officer of any standing or indeed any person who had borne arms or assisted those under arms could expect no mercy in the immediate aftermath of the battle, and flight was the only option.

The Oliphants, father and son, took refuge in the Angus glens and for the next seven months managed to evade capture. They were able to safely take ship from Arbroath to Amsterdam on 5 No-vember 1746 and from thence to Sweden. Eventually they found their way to France where they held unfulfilled hopes of a pen-sion from King Louis XV, whilst back in Scotland the house and lands of Gask were attainted and handed over to the Hanoverian Exchequer.

By 1753 however, a cousin, Laurence Oliphant of Condie, and various other relatives including Ebenezer Oliphant the goldsmith, were able to buy the lands back for £16,000, with the property being placed in the ownership of Laurence Senior's wife, Lady Gask, the debt being paid off by the sale of a small proportion of the land, and by 1763 all the exiles were able to return home.

The life of a Jacobite exile after Culloden is a story of disappointment and frustration, borne by and large with fortitude. Those who were able offered their swords to whoever might have need of them and in a position to pay and the few who were lucky enough to receive a French pension were able to survive in France. Such a one was Henry Nairne, 8th son of the 3rd Lord Nairne and uncle to Carolina's future husband William Nairne. Born on 1 November

Henry Nairne, 1727-1818.

1727, he had joined the Jacobite army in 1745 at Blair Castle and served throughout the campaign as one of Prince Charles's ADC's along with Carolina's father Laurence. After Culloden he had escaped, along with his father and the Oliphant father and son, to Sweden and then France, and had remained part of Prince Charles's entourage right up until the latter's death on 31 January 1788 at the Palazzo Muti in Rome.

Henry served as an officer in the French army, had for a time a small French pension, and his latter years were spent back in Scotland, in Perth, where he was a regular visitor at the house of Carolina's sister May and her husband Alexander Stewart. Though living in relative poverty he became a well-known figure in Perth with his antiquated French court costume of green satin, tales of times past, and general good humour. He died in 1818.

In many ways, despite this life of considerable disappointment, he was one of the luckier ones, being of the officer elite. The contemporary divisions in loyalty amongst his rank are well illustrated within his own immediate family. His two eldest brothers and two sisters were all dead by 1737 and of his remaining five brothers Thomas and Charles were fellow Jacobites, with the latter serving in the Dutch army whilst the eldest surviving brother John, Carolina's father-in-law, was serving with the British government forces. And of his three uncles, Robert, an ardent Jacobite, was killed at Culloden, William was the captain of an East Indiaman merchant ship lost off St Helena in 1743, and James was an officer in the British army. But his eight aunts were all staunchly Jacobite and indeed the eldest, Margaret, wife of William Drummond Viscount Strathallan, was imprisoned in Edinburgh Castle in 1746 though later released.

The death of Prince Charles in 1788 in effect brought to an end the flickering flame of Jacobitism and the French Revolution of the following year did the same for any remaining Jacobite pensions from the French king. But by this time quite a number of Scots Jacobites had settled in France and the upheavals of the 1790s opened

Amelia Nairne, 1698-1774, Carolina's grandmother.

the door for considerable success. One of the most notable figures would be Étienne Jacques MacDonald, son of Neil MacEachen (later MacDonald) from Howbeg in South Uist. Neil, tutor to the Clanranald family and a staunch Jacobite, was a close relative of Flora MacDonald and along with her played a key role in Prince Charles's escape from Scotland in 1746. He was amongst the Prince's entourage during this escape to France, where he married a French laundress and lived in considerable poverty at Sancerre.

Their son Jacques, however, joined the Irish Legion in the French Army, took the revolutionary side, and was, under Napoleon, to become a Marshall of France and Duke of Taranto. It's worth noting though that despite entrusting him with large independent commands Bonaparte ensured that Marshall MacDonald would never be within earshot of the sound of the bagpipes, for fear his ancestral predilictions might reassert themselves.

Along with Neil MacEachen there are many tales of extreme poverty amongst Jacobite exiles in the aftermath of Culloden, particularly from the lower ranks, and the Oliphants, though far from well-off, found themselves frequently called on to assist as they could. The family lived mostly at Corbeil in the region of Versailles and that is where, in 1755, Laurence Junior married his first cousin, Margaret or Meggy Robertson of Strowan, daughter of Duncan Robertson of Strowan who had become Chief of the Clan Donnachaidh in 1749. Their mothers, Amelia and Marjory, were sisters and daughters of the 2nd Lord Nairne and all were exiles together. Meggy was only sixteen and of striking beauty, and it is interesting to note her father's comments on his new in-laws: 'I don't know another family on earth' writes Strowan, 'to whom I would have given my child without asking some previous questions, as there are but few that have principles to supply the place of bargains.'

He is referring to religious as well as political principles and the Strowan and Gask families held very similar views to one another in this regard. 'I earnestly entreat you, my dear daughter,' wrote her father to Meggy prior to the wedding, 'to have your Bible often in your hand, and let the dictates of it remain eternally engraved upon your heart.' He continues, 'This will give you double satisfaction in prosperity; making adversity light, your amusements innocent, your mirth free from folly, and your conversation inoffensive. You are desired in marriage by a gentleman who knows that you have no fortune. What can be his inducement? Probably, indeed, he sees something agreeable in your person; but that is not the main point; it is this – he himself has been brought up in the paths of honour and virtue, in which he resolves to persist. He has a favourable opinion of your temper and education, and expects to find in you an agreeable companion for life. I have not the least reason to think he will be disappointed; you have a mother's example, and I thank God you have a moderate share of common sense; and I may tell you for once that you advance in discretion as in years; but, alas! those years are so few, and your experience so little, that I give you another half-sheet of such directions as I think may be of use to you.'

And on he goes with considerably more than a 'half-sheet' of instructions and concludes:

> What I have written I beg you will read over and over again. My daughter, as the wife of Mr. Oliphant, claims a double regard. I pray God that you may be a comfort to him, and the instrument of happiness to his family.

Laurence and Meggy's first child, a son named of course Laurence, was born rather surprisingly in London a year later in 1756, and it appears that it was possible for family members of exiled Jacobites to travel back to Britain, though usually in some incognito form, on a reasonably regular basis. Indeed Laurence's mother Amelia (Amélie), who accompanied her daughter-in-law on this occasion, had made several journeys back and forth before this one. During the journey to England the pregnant Meggy survived a coach crash near Beauvais, took to horseback behind her husband who was accompanying her to the coast and almost immediately fell off, and after that had to walk on a stiflingly hot day. They endured a stormy crossing from Boulogne followed by a flat calm off Deal for six hours and then on the coach journey to London there were two alarms concerning highwaymen. Amazingly they seem to have survived unscathed and reached their destination in London without further mishap. After the birth they returned to France and lived in Paris, but sadly the baby Laurence was not to survive a year. In the words of his grandfather:

> October 8th 1757 - At half ane hour after six in the morning, the Dear Boy my grandson Laurence Oliphant dyed

. . . All these distempers seem's to have proceeded from teething: four appear'd the week before he dyed and other five were pushing but he fail'd in strength to bring them out. I grudge much that he got not in time Medecines. He was buried in the Church of St Jacques in Corbeil.

Meggy was only seventeen and both she and her husband found this blow hard to recover from. They eventually did but it took some years and further family did not follow until a return to Scotland five years later.

2
'Kind He'rts Were Dwellin' there'

BY 1760 antagonism in Britain to the Jacobite exiles was beginning
to ease. In 1762 Meggy Oliphant was once more pregnant and it was
decided that she and her mother-in-law should return to Scotland
so that the expected heir might be born there. This they were safely
able to do thanks in part at least to the good offices of a fellow Scot
and family friend, the famous anatomist Doctor William Hunter,
who used his extensive contacts and good position (he was about to
become personal physician to Queen Charlotte) to ensure safe and
comfortable journeys and accommodation for the Oliphant ladies
as they travelled home through England. Gask was safely reached
and in the Journal of Laurence Oliphant Snr. we find the following:

> 1762, October 22 – On this day my Daughter in law was
> brought to bed of a Daughter at Gask; christened by Mr.
> Erskine, Minister at Muthil, Marjory Ann Mary.

The following year the Oliphant men decided it was time to
take a risk and return home as well. By now the de facto British
Prime Minister was Lord Bute, favourite of George III, and it may
be that they reasoned that the influential presence of a relatively
benign countryman would ease the way. The first to travel was Lau-
rence the younger, under the name of 'Mr. Brown', and his father
followed shortly afterwards using the name of 'Whytt'. Perthshire
was safely reached and a new chapter in their lives was to begin.

Life at Gask was of necessity very quiet for the next few years,
with the Oliphants seeing only their closest friends and never stray-
ing far from their own hearth. Laurence and Meggy did in fact re-
turn to France for a brief continental trip in 1768 that was under-
taken in an effort to improve his health. They were able during this

Laurence Oliphant, 1724-92, 7th Laird of Gask, Carolina's father.

trip to spend some days in Rome and dine on one evening with their 'King'. At this time the Oliphant menfolk were still nominally at risk from informers, particularly the old Laird as an 'attainted rebel', but it is perhaps consequent on this that they were able to create and foster a home life that meant so much to the ever-growing family of the younger Laurence and his Meggy. Their second daughter Amelia was born in 1765, Carolina a year later, Laurence in 1768, Margaret in 1770, and Charles in 1772. Carolina is reported to have been quite fat in her early years, 'a sturdy tod' as her mother Meggy put it. Writing to Carolina's Strowan grandmother, still in exile at Givet in France, she continues:

Meggy Oliphant (Margaret Robertson of Strowan), 1739-74,
Carolina's mother, by Sir John Watson Gordon.

You would have been pleased had you seen my little woman sitting on a chair, as prim as any there, at the reading this evening, being Sunday. Understand she cannot, but keeps her eye generally fixed on her papa, whom they are all very fond of, as they get sense.

Letter-writing was the norm for a family such as the Oliphants, and the children were introduced to it at an early age. Here is one of the first letters that Carolina was to receive, written to her by her sister May (Marjory), then aged eleven, from Lisbon in December 1773:

Dr Carolina, – I wrote to Ame last and will to Laurence next. We have been in the King's Gardens which are finely ornamented with orange and lemone trees, and walls in their hygest Bouty though no flowers.

I am your aft. sister, MO.*

The old Laird, who had been created 'Lord Oliphant' by his 'King' in 1760, died in 1767 and, in the words of his son:

My dear Father, of twelve days Illness. In his life God was gratious to him, and at Death made his passage easy; a fond father and a good man, he got his wish to be gathered to his Fathers and if it be permitted to departed spirits, he still watches over his family.

Meggy herself fell ill in 1773 and she, her husband Laurence, and their eldest daughter May embarked on another overseas trip in a misguided effort to find an improvement in her health. At this point the children were for a year in the care of their grandmother, old Lady Gask (Amelia Oliphant), and a governess named Mrs Cramond. Lady Gask's sisters, Mary and Henrietta (Harriet), were also living in the house at this time, but both Lady Gask and Mary fell ill almost simultaneously in February 1775, with Mary dying on 2 March and her sister sixteen days later. This was before Laurence and Meggy had returned home.

Henrietta took over looking after the family and was to remain with them until her death at 89 years of age in 1802. It seems that much of the fun in the household was to come from Henrietta whose child-rearing attributes were perhaps not stern by the standards of the day, and clearly the children, and Carolina in particular, were willing

*The King of Portugal's stone-built palace and gardens had been destroyed in the Lisbon earthquake of 1755 and a wooden structure had been put up in its place.

Marjorie (May) Oliphant (Mrs Stewart of Bonskeid), 1762-1819,
Carolina's eldest sister.

and lively accomplices. It was a happy household with singing, danc-
ing, sewing, embroidery, school and music lessons, poetry, sketching
and painting. Outdoors fearless horse-riding round the countryside
seems to have been the norm and once again Carolina more than
held her own amongst her brothers and sisters. Wherever they went
it seems that all were well-regarded and liked throughout the locality.

Overall and throughout this time there were two overriding
influences on the family, one of Christian religion and the other of
duty and affection towards the Royal House of Stuart. As with many
of their kind the Oliphants were Protestants of the Episcopal persua-
sion and daily devotions were the norm at Gask. Indeed Carolina's
sister Amelia has left twelve small volumes in which she daily notes
down her efforts to maintain the highest of standards of religious
observance and laments the tiniest of failures in her concentration
on this and her behaviour throughout each day. It was a sheltered life

and all were brought up with a firm and staunch adherence to the Christian beliefs of their forebears, but it must be said that, though it might appear a fairly narrow interpretation of religion by today's standards, in Carolina's generation it was at least marked by a generosity of spirit and action that becomes particularly noticeable in Carolina herself in her later years.

Mr Erskine, the local Episcopalian minister at nearby Muthil, was a frequent visitor and all in the family displayed a deep trust in their beliefs. This is well illustrated when Meggy, Carolina's mother, fell terminally ill in 1774 after the hazardous and lengthy journey home from the visit to Portugal, Spain, France and Italy. Her communications home during this trip were almost all in verse:

> Long was it dark before they reach the Inn
> Of Vendas Novas, where new scenes begin;
> The loft, where without bedsteads they must ly,
> Was damp all o'er, and not since washing dry.

And she continues in this vein for some considerable length, ninety verses in all. Sadly her health did not improve on returning home. Hers appears to have been a respiratory illness which she faced with bravery and no complaint. In her husband's words:

> She talked to me of death and our future meeting as if only going a journey for health. She called for all the children, took leave of them without the least emotion, said, as they were going away, 'See who will be the best bairn and stay most with Papa.' She said, 'You see how easily I can part with the bairns, for I know they are in good hands,' meaning their Maker.

And 'best bairns' they were, and the four girls, unmarried though not short of suitors, remained with their father and looked

The Auld Hoose o' Gask.

after him right up until his death in 1792. And his two sons did likewise and did not embark on life or careers away from home until that time.

Another trait associated with this upbringing is that of modesty, and all displayed it in one way or another, with Carolina once again taking it to a particular extreme in terms of her songwriting and acts of generosity. The life at Gask was encapsulated by Carolina when she was much older in her warm and loving tribute to the place and its people:

The Auld Hoose

> Oh the auld hoose, the auld hoose,
> What tho' the rooms were wee;
> Kind herts were dwellin' there
> And bairnies fu' o' glee.
> The wild rose and the jessamine
> Still hung upon the wa',

How mony cherish'd memories
Do they, sweet floo'ers, reca'.

Oh the auld laird, the auld laird,
Sae canty, kind and crouse,
How mony did he welcome tae
His ain wee dear auld hoose;
And the leddy too, sae genty,
There sheltered Scotland's heir,
And clipt a lock wi' her ain hand
Frae his lang yellow hair.

The mavis still does sweetly sing,
The blue bells sweetly blaw,
The bonny Earn's clear winding still,
But the auld hoose is awa'.
The auld hoose, the auld hoose,
Deserted tho' ye be,
There ne'er can be a new hoose
Will seem sae fair tae me.

Still flourishing the auld pear tree
The bairnies liked tae see,
And oh, how often did they speir
When ripe they a' wad be?
The voices sweet, the wee bit feet
Aye rinnin' here and there,
The merry shout – oh! whiles we greet
Tae think we'll hear nae mair.

For they are a' wide scattered noo,
Some tae the Indies gane,

THE AULD HOUSE

FROM

LAYS OF STRATHEARN.

Symphonies & Accompaniments

By Elizabeth Rainforth

14

15

And ane alas! tae her lang hame
Not here we'll meet again.
The kirkyaird, the kirkyaird,
Wi' floo'ers o' every hue,
Shelter'd by the holly's shade
And the dark sombre yew.

The setting sun, the setting sun,
How glorious it ga'ed doon;
The cloudy splendour raised our he'rts
Tae cloudless skies aboon.
The auld dial, the auld dial,
It tauld how time did pass;
The wintry winds hae dung it doon,
Now hid 'mang weeds and grass.

This simple tribute transcends the particular and will surely resonate for as long as there are homes to be fondly remembered.

The other thread through life at Gask was that adherence to the 'king o'er the water' and all that it entailed. Healths to the 'king' were frequently proposed but the name of the king in question began with a capital C and the London incumbents were referred to only as K and Q. At this distance this might seem trivial and faintly humorous but it must be remembered that to begin with, at any rate, a toast to the wrong party could result in arrest if reported to an unsympathetic authority and for an attainted rebel such as the older Laurence, that initially might mean imprisonment or even execution. It is worth quoting from a letter written by the said king over the water in 1783 when writing to a certain Mr Cowley, Prior of English Benedictines in Paris. Charles writes:

It gives a sensible pleasure ye remembrance of Oliphant of Gask. He is as worthy a subject as I have, and his family never deroged from their principles.

Yr sincere friend,

CHARLES R.

By the time of this letter the general situation for known Jacobites had in fact become considerably easier, and not so long after this, when the Jacobite loyalty of Gask was reported to King George III, he sent the following message to the Laird of Gask via the Member of Parliament for Perthshire:

Give my compliments – not the compliments of the King of England but those of the Elector of Hanover – to Mr. Oliphant and tell him how much I respect him for the steadiness of his principles.

And besides the generosity of spirit on behalf of King George this note demonstrates the security of the House of Hanover and with it the safety of the House of Gask. Incidentally the Member for Perthshire at this time was Laurence Oliphant's cousin, James Murray, the second son of Lord George Murray, the Jacobite general, illustrating how times had changed and how convoluted and interwoven remained the fortunes of the relatively small number of families who held positions of influence and authority in each area of the country.

Christian faith of the Episcopal variety and adherence to the House of Stuart were, it seems, inextricably linked together in the Oliphant household and this is very obvious in a prayer, dated 16 August 1779, written in the Laird's own hand:

O Lord, be gratious to our King and Queen, enable the King to please thee and shine forth an example in Virtue.

May he be the Instrument in thy hands of restoring truth and justice to these Nations and of turning many thousands unto thee. May all his Subjects become dutyfull and obedient unto him; and all our pass'd Iniquitys be pardoned. May the neighbouring Nations joyn, and kindly all events concur to bring the King back. May the present Possessor think upon his ways, do justice to the King, and have thy favour upon him and his family for doing so. But upon the King's head may the Crown flowerish, and may he live with the Queen in virtue, comfort, and affection, be blessed with children, and whatever be thy will here, made greatly happy hereafter for our Saviour's sake. Amen.

There's no doubting the sincerity of this invocation but it is at best ironic that the said 'King', who was by this time living in Florence, was far indeed from being an 'example in Virtue'. Faithful Jacobites such as Gask did, it would seem, hear reports of the erratic and inebriated behaviour of their 'King', but these in no way dented their belief in the successful restoration of a worthy monarch. The King ruled by divine right, and though this idea is not spelt out in any of the Oliphant documents it remains an underlying tenet of their belief in and support for the Royal House of Stuart.

From being a 'sturdy tod' Carolina grew to be a tall and striking young lady, with dark eyes and hair, aquiline nose and small mouth, and a dignified air; and at the same time full of life and high spirits and particularly fond of music and dancing, much deserving of the title 'The Flower of Strathearn' that she seems to have become known by in her circle. Her elder sister Marjory, or May as she was known, had on one occasion started a letter to their Robertson (Strowan) relatives who were still living in exile at Givet in France near to the Flemish border, and Carolina interjected with the following:

Carolina Oliphant as a young woman.

As May is at present playing some favourite tunes of mine, I hope you will not expect a very correct epistle; for to hear agreeable music and at the same time employ my mind about any thing else is what I can hardly do, for

> 'Music has charm to soothe a Savage Breast,
> To soften rocks and bend the knotted Oak.'*

I do think that Music engrosses all the senses and leaves not one faculty of the Mind unemployed (so says with all her heart Carolina Oliphant).

*From *The Mourning Bride* by William Congreve (1697).

Dancing in the Gask household and in similar houses of the neighbourhood was common while the family was growing up, and fiddlers were often called upon to attend and provide the music. One such was Niel Gow from Inver by Dunkeld. He was the foremost player and composer of his day and his visits must have encouraged the young Carolina in her love of Scots song and dance. She was indeed in later years to write a song in which Gow himself is the speaker:

Since first I saw fair Inver's braes
It's longer nor langsyne,
But days o' youth are blythsome days
And aft they'll come to mind.
A cot house and a wee bit land
'Tween stately Tay and rumbling Bran,
As I hae lived a favoured man
Aneath a chieftain kind.

And I've been spared a canny time,
My days been fair and long,
When thousands pu'd in a' their prime
Lie cauld the clods among.
O Robbie Burns, whar are ye noo?
Your breast o' Highland fire was fu',
Gin I could ballads make like you
I'd dee afore my song.

Gow goes on to lament the new fashion for 'Walshes' (Waltzes) and 'Kidrills' (Quadrilles) and concludes:

But waes me, I'm no' blaming them,
To brag I wad be laith,
They ken but what they hae at hame,
It's nature wi' us baith.

Gin they had torrents tumblin' doon,
Huge rocks and wilds wi' heather broom,
And mountains risin' to the moon,
Their songs might be like ours.

This song was never in fact published but it well illustrates Carolina's sympathy with the music and dance of her native land. There is a tale of Carolina in company paying a social visit one evening to a nearby house where a dance was suggested to pass the time. On finding the company to be short of a lady to make up the required number, 'The Flower of Strathearn' dashed home on horseback at midnight to get one. Incidentally this custom of giving soubriquets or nicknames seems to have been quite common within the social circles in which the Oliphants moved. 'The Strathearn Rose' was Miss Moray of Abercairney, 'The Star of the Stormont' was Miss Murray of Kincairny, 'The Moor Pout' was Miss Drummond of Pitkellony, and there was also 'The Strathallan Trout', though fortunately for the bearer of this title it is, perhaps wisely, not recorded who this might have been.

Entertainment was sought elsewhere as well, as evinced by this letter from Carolina to her brother Laurence who had embarked on a trip to London. She writes:

> I drank tea at Inchbrakie. It would make you too vain to tell you how obligingly Miss Preston asked after you. She says she is to be here soon. I hope not till you return. Louisa Graeme, Catherine Preston, and I danced while the heiress played, and we were very merry. A friend was going to see 'Jane Shore'* acted by puppets at Crieff. We had tickets but no chaperone, so were obliged to go home

* *The Tragedy of Jane Shore* is a 1714 play by Nicholas Rowe and concerns the life of one of the mistresses of Edward IV of England.

without a laugh at the tragedy. I galloped Hercules, and like him better than Glen; but you will call me quite vulgar for bringing Crieff and its environs into your mind whilst you are shewing away in St. James' Square, London.

The Laird of Gask died on 1 January 1792, and with him went the link to an older time. His character, inclinations and hospitality were well-known throughout the area, as remarked by James Alves in his poem of 1783, 'Drummond Castle; a descriptive view of Strathern':

> Not far removed, though much obscured with wood,
> Gask's rural dwelling has for ages stood,
> Where honest Oliphant, a cheerful host,
> Still cracks his jokes, and drinks his fav'rite toast.

It has more than once been suggested that his personality formed the basis for Sir Walter Scott's character the Baron of Bradwardine in *Waverley*, with the house of Gask being the prototype for Tully-Veolan in the same novel. This is quite possible, and either he or his father, the sixth Laird, could be considered as the inspiration, given that Scott's friend William Erskine (Lord Kinedder) had known the Oliphants and Gask since his childhood in nearby Muthill. Be that as it may, the seventh Laird does not seem to have had personal enemies of any kind and there is no doubt that his benevolent charm had great influence on all his family. As his poetess daughter, Carolina, put it:

> Oh, the auld laird, the auld laird,
> Sae canty, kind and crouse,
> How mony did he welcome tae
> His ain wee dear auld hoose.

*South west view of the Auld Hoose o' Gask, 1801 watercolour by
R. Carlile.*

In fact all four of his daughters and his wife were poetesses, and
were well able to launch into rhyme on virtually any subject; and
there are many examples of this from all of them. After his passing
the family politics were to become less extreme and perhaps more
realistic. Indeed young Laurence, who now became the eighth Laird,
enlisted in the Perthshire Light Dragoons in 1794 and was commis-
sioned Captain the following year, all in the service of King George
and against the forces of democracy and change that were blowing
strong from Paris and threatening to engulf the established order
throughout Europe. It is worth noting that many Jacobites had
transferred their allegiance to the House of Hanover on the death
of their own King Charles III (Bonnie Prince Charlie) in 1788, but
not of course the Laird of Gask. So much was this the case that on
being informed by the clergyman, Mr Cruickshank, who had by this
time been conducting Episcopal services at the houses of the local

Jacobite gentry, that he was moving his allegiance, Gask wrote to him in the following terms:

July 3, 1788.

Mr. Oliphant presents his compliments to Mr. Cruickshank, and as he has incapacitated himself from officiating at Gask, his gown is sent by the carrier, and the books he gave the reading of. As Mr. Cruickshank has received his stipend to this Whitsuntide, there is no money transaction to settle between him and Mr. Oliphant.

It does not appear that this staunchness of principle was held against the Laird of Gask in any way. Indeed it was to be expected of him, given his history. One of his last journeys away from Gask was in December 1787, when he attended an annual gathering of Jacobites that took place on the birthday of their King Charles III. This meeting was held in the house of James Steuart in Cleland Gardens in Edinburgh, and among those present was Robert Burns, whose reply to the invitation to attend had come in verse form:

> Tho something like moisture conglobes in my eye,
> Let no one misdeem me disloyal,
> A poor friendless wand'rer may well claim a sigh
> Still more if that wand'rer were royal.
> My Fathers that name have revered on a throne,
> My Fathers have died to right it,
> Those Fathers would spurn their degenerate son,
> That name should he scoffingly slight it.

This was the last time they would toast him as a living monarch and it is appropriate that this would be Laurence's last excursion as well.

The whole atmosphere of her childhood at Gask clearly left a deep and lasting impression on Carolina. It was a childhood of happiness and comradeship imbued with history, loyalty and religion, and all suffused with the colours and sights of a beautiful landscape.

The Banks of the Earn

Flow sweet Earn, row sweet Earn,
Joy to a' thy bonny braes,
Spring's sweet buds aye first do blow
Where thy winding waters flow.
Thro' thy banks, which wild flowers border,
Freely wind, and proudly flow,
Where Wallace* wight fought for the right,
And gallant Grahams are lying low.

O Scotland! nurse o' mony a name
Rever'd for worth, renown'd in fame;
Let never foes tell to thy shame,
Gane is thy ancient loyalty.
But still the true-born warlike band
That guards thy high unconquer'd land,
As did their sires, join hand in hand,
To fight for law and royalty.

*In 1296 Sir William Wallace had sheltered at Gascon Ha', a building that had stood close to the site of Gask House, while being pursued and after he had beheaded one of his own followers, a certain Fawdon, who had been suspected of treachery. Fawdon's ghost appeared to Wallace and caused him to temporarily lose his mind, as reported by Blind Harry (Henry the Minstrel):

In the Gask Hall thair lugyng haif thai' tayne;
Fyre gat they sone, bot meyt than had thai nane.

(Book V, *Henry the Minstrel*)

*STRATHEARN. No. 2.

Slowly and Expressively.

Fair shone the ris_ing sky, The dew drops clad wi' mo_ny a dye,

Larks lilt_ing pib_rochs high, To wel_come day's re_turn_ing. The

spreading hills, the shad_ing trees, High wav_ing in the morning breeze;The

32

wee Scotch rose wi' sweet per _ fume, Earn's vale a _ dor _ ning.

Flow sweet Earn, row sweet Earn,
Joy to a' thy bonny braes,
Spring's sweet buds aye first do blow
Where thy winding waters flow.
Thro' thy banks, which wild flowers border,
Freely wind, and proudly flow,
Where Wallace wight fought for the right,
And gallant Grahams are lying low.

O Scotland! nurse o' mony a name
Revered for worth, renowned in fame;
Let never foes tell to thy shame,
Gane is their ancient loyalty.
But still the true born warlike bands
That guard thy high unconquered lands,
As did their sires, join hand in hand,
To fight for law and royalty.

Ne'er, ne'er for greed o' gear,
Let thy brave sons, like fugies, hide
Where lawless stills pollute the rills
That o'er thy hills and vallies glide.
While in the field they scorn to yield,
And while their native soil is dear,
O may their truth be as its rocks,
And conscience, as its waters clear.

33

Bonny Gascon* Ha'

Lane, on the winding Earn, there stands
An unco tow'r, sae stern an' auld,
Biggit by lang forgotten hands –
Aince refuge o' the Wallace bauld.

Gi'e pillar'd fame to common men,
Nae need o' cairns for ane like thee;
In ev'ry cave, wood, hill, and glen,
WALLACE! remembered aye shall be.

(Carolina Oliphant)

Carolina was to later recall her childhood and its happy home
in one of her most affecting songs:

The Rowan Tree

Oh Rowan Tree, Oh Rowan Tree, thou'lt aye be dear tae me,
Intwin'd thou art wi' mony ties o' hame and infancy.
Thy leaves were aye the first o' spring, thy flow'rs the simmer's pride;
There was nae sic a bonny tree in a' the countrie side.
      Oh Rowan Tree.

How fair wert thou in simmertime, wi' a' thy clusters white,
How rich and gay thy autumn dress, wi' berries red and bright;
On thy fair stem were mony names, which now nae mair I see,
But they're engraven on my he'rt, forgot they ne'er can be.
      Oh Rowan Tree.

We sat aneath thy spreading shade, the bairnies round thee ran,
They pu'd thy bonny berries red, and necklaces they strang;

*Gascon appears to have been the original form of Gask and is thought
to mean a swift-running burn or small river.

THE ROWAN TREE.* *

MODERATELY
SLOW
AND WITH
MUCH FEELING.

Oh! Row_an Tree, Oh! Row_an Tree! thou'lt aye be dear to me, In_

twin'd thou art wi' mo _ ny ties, o' hame and in _ fan _ cy. Thy

leaves were aye the first o' spring, Thy flow'rs the sim _ mer's pride; There

*The Mountain Ash.

118

was nae sic a' bon-ny tree, in a' the coun-trie side. Oh!

Row _ _ an tree.

2nd How
3rd We

fair wert thou in sim _ mer time, wi' a' thy clus _ ters white, How
sat a _ neath thy spread _ ing shade, the bairn _ ies round thee ran, They

rich and gay thy au _ tumn dress, wi' ber _ ries red and bright. On
pu'd thy bon _ ny ber _ ries red, and neck _ la _ ces they strang. My

119

My mother! Oh I see her still, she smil'd our sports to see,
Wi' little Jeanie on her lap, an' Jamie at her knee.
    Oh Rowan Tree.

Oh! then arose my father's prayer, in holy evening's calm,
How sweet was then my mother's voice in the Martyr's psalm;
Now a' are gane! we meet nae mair aneath the Rowan Tree,
But hallowed thoughts around thee twine o' hame and infancy.
    Oh Rowan Tree.

3
'The Fairest Flower'

IN A HOUSE filled with music, song and dance it's little to be wondered that the inhabitants should be themselves creative, and this the Oliphant family were, in the fields of music, poetry, drawing, painting, and embroidery. Carolina and her sisters were all accomplished in these areas, and many examples of their work still survive. It appears that Carolina persuaded her brother Laurence to add his name to the subscription list for the collection of Robert Burns' poems that had been announced in 1786, and shortly afterwards when Burns became a contributor to James Johnson's *Scots Musical Museum* Carolina remarks on the success of his efforts to adapt new words to tunes that had hitherto carried lyrics of a somewhat unsophisticated, indelicate or coarse nature. Not all of Burns' work would fall into that category, of course, and Carolina noted this too in later years and with forceful expression, though his truly bawdy creations are unlikely to have come under her notice.

The tunes, of course, she was familiar with from the playing of Gow and the various other fiddlers and 'scrapers' whom she had danced to, and the Scots tongue and its rich vocabulary was also something that she heard all around her in the nearby village of Clathy and beyond. On one occasion she was returning to Gask, and passing a fair at Aberuthven was surprised to see many of the folk there holding in their hands a small book with a yellow cover. This turned out to be a collection of songs and ballads of somewhat dubious content, but it seems to have led Carolina to the idea that she herself might try her hand at 'improvement' and creation, for not long afterwards at a local gathering, her brother Laurence, who was now the Laird, was able to regale his tenants with a rousing

Niel Gow, 1727-1807, fiddler and composer, by Sir Henry Raeburn.

rendition of 'The Pleughman', got as he said, 'direct from the author'. This was Carolina's version of an older song and was a decided hit. Copies were made, more copies followed, and before long it was being sung throughout central Scotland, but nowhere was it stated who its author might be.

The Pleughman

There's high and low, there's rich and poor,
    There's trades and crafts eneuch, man;
But east and west his trade's the best,
    That kens to guide the pleugh, man.

Then come, weel speed my pleughman lad,
    And hey my merry pleughman;
Of a' the trades that I do ken,
    Commend me to the pleughman.

His dreams are sweet upon his bed,
    His cares are light and few, man;
His mother's blessing's on his head,
    That tents her weel, the pleughman.

Then come, weel speed etc.

The lark sae sweet that starts to meet
    The morning fresh and new, man;
Blythe tho' she be, as blythe is he
    That sings as sweet, the pleughman.

Then come, weel speed etc.

All fresh and gay, at dawn of day,
    Their labours they renew, man;
Heaven bless the seed, and bless the soil,
    And heaven bless the pleughman.

Then come, weel speed etc.

Buoyed by this success, Carolina set about the further improvement of existing songs or even the writing of new ones with the same

THE PLEUGHMAN.

There's high and low, there's rich and poor, There's trades and crafts a _ new, man, But east and west his trade's the best, That kens to guide the pleugh, man. Then, come, weel speed my pleughman lad, And hey my mer _ ry pleugh _ _ man; Of

116

a' the trades that I do ken, Com_mend me to the pleugh _ man.

mf   *cres.*

His dreams are sweet upon his bed,
  His cares are light and few, man;
His mother's blessing's on his head,
  That tents her weel, the pleughman.
    Then, come, weel speed, &c.

The lark sae sweet, that starts to meet
  The morning fresh and new, man;
Blythe tho' she be, as blythe is he
  That sings as sweet, the pleughman.
    Then, come, weel speed, &c.

All fresh and gay, at dawn of day
  Their labours they renew, man;
Heaven bless the seed, and bless the soil,
  And heaven bless the pleughman.
    Then, come, weel speed, &c.

117

end in view, and continued to so closely guard her own identity that it was never publicly revealed till after her death. By then much misattribution had taken place and, in the popular mind at any rate, this took a very long time indeed to be satisfactorily corrected, if at all. Mainly because of this secrecy it is not possible to know when or in what order the songs were composed; and Carolina continued to hide her writing activities not just at Gask but later during her married life and in widowhood as well. It is also in certain cases difficult to tell what lines are her own originals and what are adaptations of lyrics she had come across.

Her song 'The Lass o' Gowrie' is a case in point. There are at least three published versions of the song, with the earliest being ascribed to William Reid of Glasgow in the late eighteenth century, but that is likely to have been based on an older fragment. There is also another unattributed version of which the opening verses are almost identical to Carolina's. They both begin as follows:

> 'Twas on a summer's afternoon,
> A wee afore the sun gae'd doun,
> A lassie wi' a braw new goun
>   Cam' owre the hills to Gowrie.
> The rose-bud washed in summer's shower,
> Bloom'd fresh within the sunny bower;
> But Kitty was the fairest flower
>   That e'er was seen in Gowrie.
>
> To see her cousin she cam' there,
> An' oh! the scene was passing fair;
> For what in Scotland can compare
>   Wi' the Carse o' Gowrie?
> The sun was setting on the Tay,
> The blue hills melting into grey,

The mavis and the blackbird's lay
   Were sweetly heard in Gowrie.

At this point the two versions diverge, with the unattributed one proceeding without any preamble as follows:

I praised her beauty loud an' lang,
Then round her waist my arms I flang,
And said 'My dearie, will ye gang
   To see the Carse o' Gowrie?
I'll tak' ye to my father's ha',
In yon green field beside the shaw;
I'll mak' you lady o' them a' –
   The brawest wife in Gowrie.'

Soft kisses on her lips I laid,
The blush upon her cheek soon spread;
She whispered modestly, and said,
   'I'll gang wi' ye to Gowrie.'
The auld folks soon gae their consent,
Syne for Mess John they quickly sent,
Wha tied them tae their he'rts content,
   And now she's Lady Gowrie.

Carolina's ardent suitor approaches matters in a slightly more circumspect and restrained fashion, as follows:

O lang the lassie I had woo'd,
An' truth and constancy had vow'd,
But cam' nae speed wi' her I lo'ed,
   Until she saw fair Gowrie.
I pointed to my faither's ha',
Yon bonnie bield ayont the shaw,

Sae loun' that there nae blast could blaw,
    Wad she no bide in Gowrie.

Her faither was baith glad and wae;
Her mither she wad naethin' say;
The bairnies thocht they wad get play,
    If Kitty gaed to Gowrie.
She whiles did smile, she whiles did greet,
The blush and tear were on her cheek –
She naethin' said, and hung her heid;
    But now she's Leddy Gowrie.

By and large this lyric 'improvement' that Carolina sought was less successful or certainly less popular in the long run than the best of her own original efforts. Another example would be 'Cauld kail in Aberdeen', also attributed to William Reid of Glasgow, but in this case too other variants were in existence. The best known version runs as follows:

There's cauld kail in Aberdeen,
And castocks in Strathbogie.
But yet I fear they'll cook o'er soon
And never warm the coggie.

My coggie Sirs, my coggie Sirs,
I cannot want my coggie;
I wadna gi'e my three-gir'd cap
For e'er a quine on Bogie.

This is purely and simply a drinking song but Carolina turned it on its head:
    There's cauld kail in Aberdeen,
    There's castocks in Stra'bogie.

*THE LASS O' GOWRIE.

Air — Loch Erroch side.

IN MODERATE TIME.

'Twas on a summer's af_ternoon, A wee a_fore the sun gaed doune, A las_sie wi' a braw new goune Came owre the hills to Gow _ _ rie. The rose-bud wash'd in summer's showers, Bloom'd fresh wi_thin the sun_ny bower; But Kit_ty was the fair_est flower That

88

THE WHITE ROSE OF GASK 57

ere was seen in Gow _ rie.

To see her cousin she cam' there,
An' oh! the scene was passing fair;
For what in Scotland can compare
    Wi' the Carse o' Gowrie?
The sun was setting on the Tay,
The blue hills melting into grey,
The mavis and the blackbird's lay
    Were sweetly heard in Gowrie.

O lang the lassie I had lo'ed,
An' truth and constancy had vowed,
But cam' nae speed that see I could,
    Until she saw fair Gowrie.
I pointed to my faither's ha',
Yon bonnie bield ayont the shaw,
Sae loun' that there nae blast could blaw,
    Wad she no bide in Gowrie.

Her faither was baith glad and wae;
Her mither she wad naething say;
The bairnies thocht they wad get play,
    If Kitty gaed to Gowrie.
She whiles did smile, she whiles did greet,
The blush and tear was on her cheek —
She naething said, an' hung her head;
    But now she's Leddy Gowrie.

89

And, morn and e'en, they're blyth and bein,
That haud them frae the cogie.

Now haud ye frae the cogie lads,
O bide ye frae the cogie,
I'll tell ye true, ye'll never rue,
O' passin' by the cogie.

Her version continues with the story of a newly-wed husband falling into drink and as a result finally falling into the River Bogie, surviving with broken bones, and vowing never to touch a drop again. It concludes:

And ay the sang thro' Bogie rang,
O haud ye frae the cogie;
The weary gill's the sairest ill
On braes o' fair Stra'bogie.

There are several versions of this song, one of which is attributed to Carolina's contemporary the Duke of Gordon, but hers is the only one that takes a stand against the 'cogie' or drinking cup and its contents.

Collections of folk song were now more readily available than earlier in the eighteenth century and were being continually added to as Carolina was growing up, and songs and poems in Scots were being written, so one can understand with the family's general poetic interests why she would become involved in such an activity. Generally speaking the earlier part of the eighteenth century had in literary terms been more concerned with prose, but the era of Addison, Johnson, Burke, Gibbon and Hume was to give way to poetry and the imagination and the era of Cowper, Burns, Wordsworth, Byron and Scott. Huge social changes in industry and agriculture were under way, new ideas were being generated through political upheaval in France and North America, and Scotland's capital was pulsating with new thought and creativity. The world was ready to improve and update and Carolina was equally ready to do her bit as she saw it.

It would however be quite incorrect to assume that her efforts would go along with a stony-faced desire to discourage enjoyment. Humour and joie-de-vivre were essential and integral parts of her early character and this she reflected in her writing. One of her earliest songs is 'The County Meeting':

> Ye're welcome, leddies, ane and a',
> Ye're welcome to our County Ha',
> Sae weel ye look, when buskit braw,
> To grace our County Meeting!
> An', gentlemen, ye're welcome too
> In waistcoats white and tartan too,
> Gae seek a partner, mak' yere bow,
> Syne dance our County Meeting.
>
> There's the Major, and his sister too,
> He in the bottle-green, she in the blue;
> (Some years sin' syne that gown was new,
> At our County Meeting.)
> They are a worthy, canty pair,
> An' unco proud o' their nephew Blair;
> O' sense, or siller, he's nae great share,
> Tho' he's the King o' the Meeting.

And the description, with the back of the hand asides, continues:

> There's beauty Bell, wha a' surpasses,
> An' heaps o' bonnie, country lasses;

Wi' the heiress o' the Gowden Lee,
Folk say she's unco dorty.
Lord Bawbee, aye, he's lookin' there,
An' sae is the Major, and Major's heir,
Wi' the Laird, the Shirra, and mony mair,
I could reckon them to forty.

See Major O'Neill has got her hand,
An' in the dance they've ta'en their stand;
(Impudence comes frae Paddy's land,
Say the lads o' our County Meeting.)
But ne'er ye fash! gang thro' the reel –
The Country-dance, ye dance sae weel –
An' ne'er let Waltz or dull Quadrille
Spoil our County Meeting.

Afore we end, strike up the spring
O' Thulichan and Hieland-fling,
The Haymakers, and Bumpkin fine!
At our County Meeting.
Gow draws his bow, folk haste away,
While some are glad and some are wae;
A' blythe to meet some ither day,
At our County Meeting.

And a bit of good-humoured fun at the expense of the next
county was never going to be taken amiss:

The Fife Laird

Ye should na' ca' the Laird daft, tho' daft-like he may be;
Ye should na' ca' the Laird daft, he's just as wise as me;
Ye should na' ca' the Laird daft, his bannet has a bee –
He's just a wee bit Fifish, like some Fife Lairds that be.

The inspiration for this song was the story of a Fife Laird's abortive attempt to pay a visit to Edinburgh by sea and how he attributed blame for his lack of success. The tune is titled 'The Fife Hunt' and would have been the obvious vehicle for the lyric to Carolina:

Last Lammas when the Laird set out to see Auld Reekie's toun,
The Firth it had nae waves at a', the waves were sleepin' soun';
But wicked witches bide about gude auld St Andrew's toun,
And they steered up an unco' blast our ain dear Laird to droun.

Afore he got to Inchkeith Isle the waves were white and hie –
'O weel I ken thae witches wud hae aye a spite at me!'
They drove him up, they drove him doon, the Fife touns a' they pass,
And up and round Queensferry toun, then doun unto the Bass.

The sailors row, but row in vain, Leith's port they canna win –
Nae meat or beds they hae on board, but there they maun remain;
O mirk and cauld the midnight hour, how thankfu' did they see
The first blush o' the dawnin' day, fair spreadin' owre the sea.

And the Laird's belief in witchcraft as the author of his misfortune remains unshaken:

'Gae hame, gae hame' the Laird cried out, 'as fast as ye can gang.
Oh rather than wi' witches meet I'd meet an ournatang –
A' nicht and day I've been away, an' naethin' could I see.
But auld wives' cantrips on broomsticks, wild cap'ring owre the sea.

I hae na' had a mouth o' meat, nor yet had aff my claes -
Afore I gang to sea again some folk maun mend their ways.'
The Laird is hame wi' a' his ain, below the Lomond hill,
Richt glad to see his sheep again, his doukit, and his mill!

THE FIFE LAIRD

Air. The Fife Hunt.

Chorus.

Ye should na ca' the Laird daft, tho' daft like he may be— Ye should na' ca' the Laird daft he's just as wise as me— Ye should na ca' the Laird daft he's bannet has a *bee*—He's just a wee bit Fif—ish like some Fife Lairds that be— Last Lammas when the Laird set out, to see Auld Reekies toune, The

109

Firth it had nae waves at a' the waves were sleepin' soune; But wicket witches bide a bout gude

auld Saint Andrews toune, An' they steer'd up an unco blast oure aine dear Laird to droune.

*Afore he got to Inchkeith Isle, the waves were white an' hie—
"O weel I ken thae witches wud hae aye a spite at me;"
They drove him up, they drove him down the Fife tounes a' they pass,
And up and round Queensferry toune, then doune unto the Bass.
The sailors row, but row in vain, Leith port they canna win—
Nae meat or beds they hae on board, but *there* they maun remain:
O mirk and cauld the midnight hour, how thankfu' did they see
The first blush o' the dawnin' day, fair spreadin' oure the sea.
    Chorus. Ye should na ca' the Laird daft, &c.

"Gae hame, gae hame," the Laird cried out, " as fast as ye can gang,
Oh! rather than wi' witches meet, I'd meet an *ournatang*
A nicht an' day I've been away, an naething could I see,
But auld wives' cantrips on broomsticks, wild cap'ring owre the sea.
I ha'e na had a mouth o' meat, nor yet had aff my claes—
Afore I gang to sea again some *folk* maun mend their ways;"
The Laird is hame wi' a' his ain, below the Lomon hill,
Richt glad to see his sheep again, his douket, and his mill!
    Chorus Ye should na ca' the Laird daft. &c.

*Begin each verse to the same part of the tune as the chorus.

Humour seems never to have been far from Carolina in her earlier songs. A young lady becoming unexpectedly heir to a fortune and the consequent shift in social and amorous attitudes towards her would have been a spectacle she had probably witnessed and most certainly heard about:

The Heiress

I'll no' be had for naething,
　　I'll no' be had for naething.
I'll tell ye, lads, that's ae thing
　　So ye needna follow me.

Oh the change is most surprising,
　　None o' them e'er looked at me;
Now my charms they're a' admiring.
　　For my sake they're like to dee.

The laird, the shirra, and the doctor,
　　And twa-three lords o' high degree;
Wi' heaps o' writers I could mention,
　　Surely, sirs, it is no' me.

But there's ane, when I had naething,
　　A' his he'rt he gi'ed to me;
And sair he toiled to mak a wee thing
　　To gie me when he cam' frae sea.

And if e'er I marry ony,
　　He will be the lad for me;
For oh, he was baith gude and bonny,
　　And he thocht the same o' me.

*THE HEIRESS.

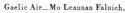

Gaelic Air—Mo Leannan Faluich.

IN MODERATE TIME.

I'll no be had for nae _ thing, I'll no be had for nae _ thing, I tell ye, lads, that's ae _ thing, So ye need na fol _ low me. Oh the change is most sur _ pris _ ing; Last year I was Bet _ sy Brown; Now

60

to my hand they're a' as_pir_ing, The fair E_liz_a I am grown!

Oh! the change is most surprising,
  Nane o' them e'er look'd at me;
Now my charms they're a' admiring,
  For my sake they're like to dee!
    But I'll no, &c.

The Laird, the Shirra, and the Doctor,
  And twa-three Lords o' high degree;
Wi' heaps o' writers, I could mention,
  Surely, sirs, it is no me!
    But I'll no, &c.

But there is ane, when I had naething,
  A' his heart he gied to me;
And sair he toiled, to mak a wee thing,
  To gie me when he cam frae sea.
    Sae I'll no, &c.

And if e'er I marry ony,
  He will be the lad for me;
For oh he was baith gude and bonny,
  And he thocht the same o' me.
    Sae I'll no, &c.

61

Carolina could always mix wit and wisdom with the best of them, and her songs and in particular the earlier ones were guaranteed to spread common sense and good cheer. So when 'The Flower of Strathearn' articulated sentiments like those in the next song she was sure to be met with nothing but hearty agreement, even though the readers or listeners would be unaware of the author's identity.

The Bonniest Lass in A' the Warld

Now lasses a' keep a gude he'rt,
Nor envy e'er a comrade,
For be ye're e'en black, blue, or grey,
Ye're bonniest aye to some lad.
The tender heart, the cheering smile,
The truth that ne'er will falter,
Are charms that never can beguile,
And time can never alter.

4
'His Very Name Our Heart's Blood Warms.'

It seems probable that her Jacobite songs were among Carolina's earliest work. Jacobite lore, relics, people, and stories were all around her and it's likely that she felt moved to write in this vein under the influence of her father and her Strowan uncle Alexander Robertson. She was, after all, a true daughter of her House. There does not seem to be any mention however of her songs being sung at Gask during her father's lifetime, nor does he refer to them at any point in his writings.

The songs themselves make use of some of the best of old Scots melodies, to the point where the song titles have now completely obliterated the old tune titles which are mostly now forgotten. Carolina would have heard the complete tale of the '45 Rising from the vantage point of first-hand experience and knowledge and her songs run from the very beginning with 'Wha'll be King but Chairlie':

> The news frae Moidart cam' yestreen
>> Will soon gar mony ferlie;
> For ships o' war hae just come in
>> And landit Royal Chairlie.

> Come thro' the heather, around him gether,
>> Ye're a' the welcomer early;
> Around him cling wi' a' your kin,
>> For wha'll be king but Chairlie?

> Come thro' the heather, around him gether,
>> Come Ronald, come Donald, come a' thegither,

Charles Edward Stuart, 1720-88, by Antonio David, 1732.

And crown your rightfu', lawfu' king,
  For wha'll be king but Chairlie?

Then here's a health to Chairlie's cause,
  And be't complete an' early;
His very name our heart's blood warms;
  To arms for Royal Chairlie!

THE WHITE ROSE OF GASK

'Charlie's Landing' too conveys the sense of excitement for those caught up in the event:

> O lang we've prayed to see this day,
>   True he'rts they maist were breaking;
> Now clouds and storms will flee away,
>   Young hope again is waking.
> We'll sound the Gathering, lang an' loud,
>   Your friends will greet ye fairlie;
> Tho' now they're few, their he'rts are true,
>   They'll live or die for Chairlie.

'Charlie is My Darling' is a good example of a song that came in a number of printed versions, with that of Burns in James Johnson's *Scots Musical Museum* (1787–1803) being perhaps the earliest, and followed by versions from James Hogg ('The Ettrick Shepherd'), and somewhat later, Captain Charles Gray. But Carolina's, and the tune that goes with it in the *The Scottish Minstrel* (1821–24), is probably the best known:

> 'Twas on a Monday morning,
>   Right early in the year,
> When Charlie came to our toun,
>   The young Chevalier.
> O Charlie is my darling,
>   My darling, my darling,
> Charlie is my darling,
>   The young Chevalier.
>
> As he came marching up the street
>   The pipes played loud an' clear;
> And a' the folk came running out
>   To meet the Chevalier.

THE WEE BOATIE or CHARLIE'S LANDING AT BARODALE.

Air—When wild wars.

In MODERATE TIME.

There cam a wee boat_ie owre the sea, Wi' the winds an' waves it strove sair _ ly; But oh! it brought great joy to me, For wha was there but Prince Char _ lie. The wind was hie, an' un _ co chill, An' a' thing luik _ et

bare _ ly; But oh we cam wi' right good will, To wel _ come

bon _ nie Char _ lie.

Waes me, puir lad, ye're thinly clad,
    The waves yere fair hair weeting;
We'll row ye in a tartan plaid,
    An' gie ye Scotland's greeting.
Tho' wild an' bleak the prospect round,
    We'll cheer yere heart, dear Charlie;
Ye're landed now on Scottish grund,
    Wi' them wha lo'e ye dearly.

O lang we've prayed to see this day;
    True hearts they maist were breaking;
Now clouds, an' storms, will flee away,
    Young Hope again is waking.
We'll sound the Gathering, lang an' loud,
    Your friends wi' joy will greet ye;
Tho' now they're few,—their hearts are true,
    They'll lieve or dee for ye, Charlie.

65

Wi' Hieland bonnets on their heads,
      And claymores bright and clear,
   They came to fight for Scotland's right,
      And the young Chevalier.

Carolina often makes a definite connection between the restoration of the House of Stuart and the restoration of Scotland's Parliament and independence, and there's no doubt that many Scottish Jacobites did clearly feel that if the Stuarts were restored the one would follow the other. But there is no reason to suppose that such a thing would have come to pass if the Cause had indeed been successful. The actions of 'The Young Pretender's' predecessors would rather indicate the opposite. The Stuarts believed that they ruled by 'Divine Right' and do not seem to have been particularly keen on any kind of parliament. But it was perhaps not an important issue by the time Carolina came to write her songs. She was more concerned with the human emotions involved than theoretical ideas of kingship and politics.

   The Whigs may scoff, the Whigs may jeer,
   But ah! that love maun be sincere,
   Which still keeps true whate'er betide,
   An' for his sake leaves a' beside.
      ('He's ower the hills that I lo'e weel')

Two further songs that concerned the campaign are without doubt from Carolina's own pen. In the first of these, 'The Hundred Pipers', she engages in a bit of poetic licence in that some of the events she describes actually took place on the retreat north rather than the earlier southern advance:

   Wi' a hundred pipers, an' a', an' a',
   Wi' a hundred pipers, an' a', an' a',
   We'll up and gi'e them a blaw, a blaw,

THE HUNDRED PIPERS.

Arranged expressly for this Edition.

113

Wi' a hundred pipers an' a', an' a'.
O it's owre the Border awa', awa',
It's owre the Border awa', awa',
We'll on and we'll march to Carlisle Ha',
Wi' its yetts, its castell, an' a', an' a'.

The Esk was swollen, sae red and sae deep,
But shouther to shouther the braw lads keep;
Twa thousand swam ower to fell English ground,
An' danced themselves dry to the pibroch's sound.
Dumbfounder'd, the English saw – they saw –
Dumbfounder'd, they heard the blaw, the blaw;
Dumbfounder'd, they a' ran awa', awa'
From the hundred pipers an' a', an' a'.

And then on to the final plaintive 'Will ye no' come back again',
when Carolina shows her ability to match one of the most poignant
of melodies with a simple, moving and yet forceful lyric:

Bonnie Chairlie's noo awa',
    Safely o'er the friendly main;
Mony a he'rt will brak in twa'
    Should he ne'er come back again.

Will ye no' come back again?
    Will ye no' come back again?
Better lo'ed ye canna be,
    Will ye no come back again!

English bribes were a' in vain,
    An' e'en tho' puirer we may be;
Siller canna buy the he'rt
    That beats aye for thine and thee.

We watched thee in the gloaming hour,
    We watched thee in the morning grey;
Tho' thirty thousand pounds they'd gie,
    O there's nane that wad betray.

Sweet the laverock's note and lang,
    Lilting wildly up the glen;
But aye to me he sings ae song,
    Will ye no come back again.

Perhaps it was necessary and easy to be a little sentimental and rosy-eyed when the real danger was past, and particularly when the subject of this veneration was by the time of his death in 1788 very far from being admirable, but it is a remarkable fact that a reward of thirty thousand pounds, at least £3.5m in today's currency, failed to lure a single betrayer from amongst a people whose entire way of life was so deeply affected by this very loyalty; this was something indeed to take pride in.

A pastoral in which the reference is more oblique, and one that appears to look back from a slightly later time, has a tone of resignation as though the singer knows that the longed-for wish may never come true:

The White Rose o' June*

Now the bricht sun, and the soft summer showers,
Deck a' the woods and the gardens wi' flowers –
But bonny and sweet tho' the hale o' them be,
There's ane aboon a' that is dearest to me,
And O, that's the white rose, the white rose o' June,
An' may he that should wear it come back again soon.

*The white rose was the emblem of the Jacobites.

WILL YE NO COME BACK AGAIN.

In MODERATE TIME.

Bon _ nie Char _ lie's now a _ wa; Safe _ ly owre the friend _ ly main; Mony a heart will break in twa, Should he ne'er come back a _ gain.

Cho: Will ye no come back a _ gain? Will ye no come back a _ gain?

22

Bet _ ter lo'ed ye can _ na be _ Will ye no come

back a _ gain?

Ye trusted in your Hieland men,
　　They trusted you, dear Charlie!
They kent your hiding in the glen,
　　Death or exile braving.
Cho!　Will ye no, &c.

English bribes were a' in vain,
　　Tho' puir, and puirer, we maun be;
Siller canna buy the heart
　　That beats aye for thine and thee.
Cho!　Will ye no, &c.

We watched thee in the gloaming hour,
　　We watched thee in the morning grey;
*Tho' thirty thousand pound they gie,
　　Oh there is nane that wad betray!
Cho!　Will ye no, &c.

Sweet's the Laverock's note and lang,
　　Lilting wildly up the glen;
But aye to me he sings ae sang,
　　Will ye no come back again?
Cho!　Will ye no, &c.

*A fact highly honourable to the Highlanders.

23

Mair fragrant and rich the red rose may be,
But there is nae spell to bind it to me –
But dear to my heart and to fond memorie,
Tho' scathed and tho' blighted the white rose may be,
O the white rose, the white rose, the white rose o' June,
O may he that should wear it come back again soon.

One aspect of Carolina's songwriting in a Jacobite connection worth noting is the question of language. The predominant speech of the Scottish Jacobite armies was Gaelic; their leaders from the north were by and large fluent Gaelic speakers and many would use it in preference to English. But English and Scots was the speech of the lowland Perthshire lairds, and there is no reference to Gaelic ever being spoken at Gask at around this time. Carolina's Strowan relatives were Gaelic speakers, and indeed Alexander Robertson, Chief of the clan until his death in 1749 and who took part in the Risings of 1689, 1715 and 1745, was a Gaelic poet of some significance and generally referred to as the Poet Chief. But certainly by the time of Carolina's generation, fluency in Gaelic does not appear to have been amongst her own family's accomplishments, though they do show familiarity with aspects of the language and its culture. Of course there were plenty of Jacobite songs and lyrics in English and Scots and Carolina was continuing that tradition. What marks her out is her innate ability to marry a simple and meaningful lyric with melody of a similar tone, thus achieving a unity which is the mark of all great song. Scots and English were also interchangeable, which greatly assisted the mechanics of songwriting and she most certainly made use of this flexibility.

It would be a mistake to think that Carolina had nothing but rose-tinted spectacles through which to view all things Jacobite. She was well aware of the human misery involved in the conflict and she was never slow to sympathise and in particular to take the female part:

The Lass of Livingstane

Oh! Wha will dry the dreeping tear,
    She sheds her lane, she sheds her lane?
Or wha the bonnie lass will cheer,
    Of Livingstane, of Livingstane?
The Crown was half on Charlie's head,
    Ae gladsome day, ae gladsome day;
The lads that shouted joy to him
    Are in the clay, are in the clay.

Her waddin' gown was wyl'd and won,
    It ne'er was on, it ne'er was on;
Culloden field, his lowly bed,
    She thocht upon, she thocht upon.
The bloom has faded frae her cheek
    In youthful prime, in youthful prime;
And sorrow's with'ring hand has done
    The deed o' time, the deed o' time.

But humorous subjects there were as well, and Carolina had heard many of the stories. One of these concerned John Gray of Kinfauns, 11th Lord Gray, who was Lord Lieutenant of Perthshire during the '45 Rising and a Government man. When the Duke of Cumberland and the Government forces reached Dundee in February 1746 on their way north prior to the Battle of Culloden, Lord Gray travelled to the city to pay his respects to the Duke. He was so coldly received and felt so insulted that, being of a hot-headed and stubborn temperament, he rode home to Kinfauns Castle, resolving to set out immediately and join the Prince's army. His lady was far from keen on this plan but she knew her man and decided that a stratagem was required. Suggesting that he should bathe his feet before the long ride north (or, as in Carolina's version take a dish of

THE LASS OF LIVINGSTANE.

Oh! wha will dry the dreep _ ing tear, She sheds her lane, she sheds her lane? Or wha the bon _ nie lass will cheer, Of Liv _ ing _ stane, Of Liv _ ing _ stane? The crown was half on

46

Her waddin' gown was wyl'd and won,
  It ne'er was on, it ne'er was on;
Culloden field, his lowly bed,
  She thought upon, she thought upon.
The bloom has faded frae her cheek
  In youthfu' prime, in youthfu' prime,
And sorrow's with'ring hand has done
  The deed o' time, the deed o' time.

47

tea) she herself 'accidentally' upset a kettle of boiling water over his legs. The scalding was so bad that the unfortunate Gray was confined to his apartments for several weeks and the lands and castle of Kinfauns were safe.

Ye'll Mount, Gudeman

LAIRD
'But haste ye now haste ye for I maun be gaun,
The mare's at the yett, the bugle is blawn;
Gi'e me my bannet, it's far in the day,
I'm no' for a dish, there's nae time to stay.'

LEDDY
'Oh dear! Tak but ane, it may do ye gude.'
But what ails the woman? She surely is wud!
She's lifted the kettle, but somehow it coup'd
On the legs of the laird, wha roar'd and wha loup'd.

LAIRD
'I'm brent, I'm brent, how cam' it this way?
I fear I'll no ride for mony a day.
Send aff the men, and to Prince Charlie say,
"My hert is wi' him but I'm tied by the tae."'

5
'A Penniless Lass wi' a Lang Pedigree'

IN THE SPRING of 1786 Laurence Oliphant sat himself down in his house at Gask and composed a letter to his much-loved daughters.

> My four dear girls, you have now got the substantial parts of education – the principles of religion and loyalty, reading, writing, sewing, dancing, a little of the harpsichord, and a little French. While we live in this life of trial and passage to a better, you have the chance of marrying or living single. My own hope and wish is that we may be all soon happy in Heaven.

And he continues in the following vein:

> It requires no proof that house-wifery was the occupation women were designed principally to be employed in, nor do the men-housewives that now and then appear alter the order established by Providence for the women; it only shows a whimsical turn, or their wife's incapacity.

This point of view was normal for the time, nor was it likely to be queried. He then goes on to enumerate the various requirements for a satisfactory domestic life – 'going to bed soon and rising early . . . arrangedness in all the things about you . . . keeping accounts . . . constantly asking questions and making enquiries, and informing yourself of the best methods', and he concludes:

> But you are not to make yourselves uneasy though you do not succeed entirely to your mind in these things: the hearty endeavour is all that is required; that done, you

Margaret (Oliphant) Keith of Ravelston and Dunottar, 1770-1847,
Carolina's sister, by Sir John Watson Gordon, 1823.

need have no anxiety about an establishment through life; striving to live well you may depend on being comfortably provided for here, and made greatly happy hereafter; which God, of his infinite goodness, grant to all my dear children. –

LAU. OLIPHANT.

Dr Alexander Stewart of Bonskeid, 1753-1835, Carolina's brother-in-law.

His daughters' disagreement with these instructions was not likely. After all the Oliphant girls were of their time and would have understood financial strictures and the choices before them, nor would they have stood out against the views of a much-loved father. When he died in 1792 they had faithfully fulfilled their mother's encouragement to look after him and after that they did all indeed

THE WHITE ROSE OF GASK

marry. Marjorie or May, the eldest, wedded Dr Alexander Stewart of Bonskeid, who as a medical doctor with a busy practice in Perth and the surrounding area had attended her father during his continuing ill-health. Dr Stewart's first wife had died and tragically their only son had been the one fatality of seventy smallpox vaccinations administered by Dr Stewart himself in Perth. Amelia, the second girl, married Charles Steuart of Dalguise, and Margaret, Carolina's younger sister, married Alexander Keith of Ravelston and Dunnottar.

Carolina herself had never been short of admirers and, quite apart from those in Perthshire, there are reports of amorous interest in her from a most 'exalted' quarter as a result of a ball held in Sunderland in 1796. To set the scene, there was considerable unrest throughout the entire land around this time as ideas from France were catching on fast: 'Damnation to the King, and success to the friends of the People' was an often heard toast. In response to this the militia was raised and supporters of the status quo, and thus by definition the House of Hanover, were not slow to answer the call. Many members of once-Jacobite families were amongst these, and one such was Carolina's brother Laurence, who received a commission in the Perthshire Dragoons. The regiment had been posted to Durham and the family including Carolina had accompanied him there. Her younger brother Charles had at this time gone to France to seek an improvement in his health. Charles had remained a staunch Jacobite and had refused the Abjuration Oath in 1796. Those who took this Oath abjured all previous adherence to the House of Stuart and, for those who did, it marked a turning of the way and a chance to re-enter the ranks of establishment and preferment. In the words of his elder brother Laurence:

> I am much persecuted about Charles. I have been at much
> trouble, and have everything in train for purchasing a
> collectorship for him . . . but I understand that the oath

Carolina Oliphant, portrait miniature.

of abjuration is indispensably necessary, which Charles I
am sure would not take, nor would I desire him. He has
some idea of going into the fur trade in Canada. He would
probably get over head and ears in debt, from ignorance of
business, and I am afraid might get into a habit of tipling
with low bodies.

THE WHITE ROSE OF GASK

None of this came to pass, as sadly Charles did not find the medical improvement he was looking for. It seems that he was suffering from consumption; his health deteriorated and he died at Gask on 23 July 1797.

Prior to this, in August 1796, there had been great excitement in the north of England with the construction and opening of the Wearmouth Bridge over the River Wear, only the second iron bridge to be built in England. As part of the celebrations a ball was held and the Oliphant family, who were by now in Durham, attended. Carolina danced with a Royal Duke who is reported to have afterwards sought her hand. Such a union would probably have been prohibited by the Royal Marriage Act of 1772 under the terms of which any direct descendant of George II required the Sovereign's consent to legally marry, but the amorous Duke fell by the wayside in any case.* The Royal Dukes of the time do not appear to have been a particularly admirable group so, even if the story were true, it was perhaps just as well that Carolina had long given her heart to her second cousin William Murray Nairne, and it was only his relative poverty as a Captain in the army in Fraser's 71st Regiment that had prevented their marriage before that. In her diaries, and written in William's hand, are the verses of a song titled 'As the Thames' Rolling Stream Moved Pensive along' which William had sung on some earlier occasion at Gask, and beside these Carolina had made the following note:

Written by my desire by my then future most beloved husband when I was about 17 years old at Gask. Wished to

*The Wearmouth Bridge was opened on 9 August 1796 by H.R.H. Prince William of Gloucester, a grandson of George II. He is the likely Duke in question but was ten years Carolina's junior and only twenty at the time. As with Carolina, he married his cousin (Princess Mary, the fourth daughter of George III) and he was forty years old when he did so in 1816.

have these lines because they seemed so beautiful when he sang them.

In 1806 came a change of fortune when William was appointed Assistant Inspector-General of Barracks in Scotland, based at Edinburgh Castle and with the rank and pay of Major. The 'auld hoose' of Gask had been demolished in 1801, but a new and much grander mansion had risen in its place and the couple were married there on 2 June 1806. Carolina was 39 years old.

Carolina was clearly torn between the excitement of a beckoning new life and the home and scenes that she knew and loved so well.

Adieu to Strathearn

Strathearn, O how shall I quit thy sweet groves?
How bid thee a long, O an endless adieu.
Sad memory over such happiness roves,
As not hope's own magic can ever renew.

Sweet scene of my childhood, delight of my youth!
Thy far-winding waters no more I must see;
Thy high-waving bowers, thy gay woodland flowers,
They wave now, they bloom now, no longer for me.

And she is in similar vein in 'Her Home She Is Leaving':

To the hills of her youth, cloth'd in all their rich wildness,
Farewell she is bidding, in all her sweet mildness,
And still, as the moment of parting is nearer,
Each long-cherish'd object is fairer and dearer.
Not a grove or fresh streamlet but wakens reflection
Of hearts still and cold, that glow'd with affection;

STRATHEARN.

Air—Miss Carmichael.

Strath _ _ earn oh! how shall I quit thy sweet groves? How bid thee a long, oh! an end _ _ less a _ _ dieu? Sad mem _ o _ ry o _ ver such hap _ pi _ ness

Slow, and with Expression.

p elegato.

30

roves, As not hope's own ma _ _ gic can

ev _ er re _ new.

Sweet scene of my childhood, delight of my youth!
Thy far-winding waters no more I must see;
Thy high-waving bowers, thy gay woodland flowers,
They wave now, they bloom now, no longer for me!

31

The new house of Gask.

Not a breeze that blows over the flow'rs of the wildwood
But tells, as it passes, how blest was her childhood.

She need not have worried. The Nairnes set up home in Edinburgh in a small house on the eastern edge of Duddingston generously purchased for them by Carolina's Strowan grandfather and named Caroline Cottage. Their only child William was born in July in 1808 in a house in Hope Street in Edinburgh where they had moved to spend the winter, and the next twenty-two years were filled with a gentle happiness and contentment. In addition to Caroline Cottage one unexpected perk of William's post as Assistant Inspector of Barracks in Scotland came in the shape of the use of the Royal Apartments in Holyrood Palace, and these they were able to retain until required by the Royal household for George IV's celebrated visit to Edinburgh in 1822.

One of Carolina's best-loved and most likeable songs may well have been written some years before her marriage, but after moving to Edinburgh she would certainly have had the opportunity to visit the place in question. The tune and the title are older and this is a good example of Carolina's use of existing material as a starting-point, but no more than that. It seems likely that the original song dates from the time of Charles II and concerns one Mark Carse, who had been the owner of Cockpen in modern Midlothian. But in Carolina's song the characters are so essentially Scottish, so human, and so lightly humorous and general in application, that it matters not where she took her inspiration from. She was observant and could catch the quirkiness of both character and type with the deftest of touches, and the tune she made use of may well have put some of the ideas in her mind, titled as it was 'When She Cam' ben She Bobbit':

The Laird o' Cockpen

The Laird o' Cockpen, he's prood an' he's great,
His mind is ta'en up wi' things o' the State.
He wanted a wife, his braw hoose tae keep,
But favour wi' wooin' was fashious tae seek.

Doon by the dyke-side a lady did dwell,
At his table-heid he thocht she'd look well,
McLeish's ae dochter o' Claversha' Lee,
A penniless lass wi' a lang pedigree.

His wig was weel-poother'd and as gude as new;
His waistcot was white, his coat it was blue;
He put on a ring, a sword and cock'd hat,
An' wha' could refuse the Laird wi' a' that?

He took the grey mare, and rade cannily,
An' rapp't at the yett o' Claversha' Lee.

*THE LAIRD O' COCKPEN.

Air—When she cam' ben, she bobbed.

LIVELY.

The laird o' Cock pen, he's proud an' he's great, His mind is ta'en up wi' things o' the state; He want ed a wife his braw house to keep, But fa vour wi' woo in' was

68

fash_ous to seek.

Down by the dyke-side a lady did dwell,
At his table head he thought she'd look well,
Mᶜ Clish's ae daughter o' Claverse-ha' Lee,
A pennyless lass wi' a lang pedigree.

His wig was weel pouther'd, and as guid as new;
His waistcoat was white, his coat it was blue;
He put on a ring, a sword and cock't hat,
And wha could refuse the laird wi' a' that.

He took the grey mare, and rade cannily,
An' rapt at the yett o' Claverse-ha' Lee;
"Gae tell mistress Jean to come speedily ben,
She's wanted to speak to the laird o' Cockpen."

Mistress Jean was makin' the elder-flower wine,
"An' what brings the laird at sic a like time?"
She put aff her aprin, and on her silk gown,
Her mutch wi' red ribbons, and gaed awa down.

An' when she cam' ben he bowed fu' low,
An' what was his errand he soon let her know;
Amazed was the laird when the lady said Na,
And wi' a laigh curtsie she turned awa.

Dumfounder'd he was, nae sigh did he gie,
He mounted his mere _ he rade cannily,
And aften he thought, as he gaed thro' the glen,
She's daft to refuse the laird o' Cockpen.

69

'Gae tell Mistress Jean tae come speedily ben,
For she's wanted tae speak wi' the Laird o' Cockpen.'

Mistress Jean she was makin' the elderfloo'er wine.
'An' what brings the Laird here at sic a like time?'
She put aff her apron, put on her silk goon,
Her mutch wi' red ribbons, and ga'ed awa' doon.

An' when she cam' ben he bowed fu' low,
An' what was his errand he soon let her know;
Amazed was the Laird when the lassie said 'Na',
An' wi' a laigh curtsie she turn'd awa'.

Dumfooner'd he was but nae sigh did he gi'e,
He mounted his mare an' he rade cannily;
But often he thocht as he gaed thro' the glen,
'She was daft tae refuse the Laird o' Cockpen.'

It is interesting to note that two further verses were added at a later date but it's almost certain that these were not by Carolina herself. They run as follows:

And now that the Laird his exit had made,
Mistress Jean she reflected on what she had said;
'Oh, for ane I'll get better, it's waur I'll get ten,
I was daft to refuse the Laird o' Cockpen.'

Next time that the Laird and the lady were seen,
They were gaun arm-in-arm to the kirk on the green;
Now she sits in the Ha' like a weel-tappit hen,
But as yet there's nae chickens appear'd at Cockpen.

These verses do not appear in the original manuscript and they do seem a little clumsy in comparison to what has gone before. Nor is it likely that Carolina would have indulged in the reference to 'chickens' given her desire to improve and purify the national song. The verses have been attributed to the novelist Susan Ferrier who was an Edinburgh contemporary of Carolina's and whom she certainly knew. Of course Susan Ferrier would have had no idea of the literary accomplishments of Mrs Nairne. Unfortunately one by-product of anonymity can be that addition by other writers is not thought of as being out of place, and Carolina's work has definitely suffered from this from time to time.

6
'The Day is aye Fair'

CAROLINA'S HUSBAND, William Nairne, was nine years her senior and a popular and respected figure. His great-grandfather was the second Lord Nairne who had escaped the gallows in 1716 by the merest whisker, and his grandfather, John, third Lord Nairne, had shared the same last-minute reprieve and had gone on to take part in the 1745 Rising and thereafter had fled to France along with the Lairds of Gask. He was attainted for the second time and lost his title and lands. His house, Nairne House at Auchtergaven near Perth, was purchased from the Exchequer by the Duke of Atholl and demolished in 1748. William's father, Lt. Col. John Nairne, *de jure* the fourth Lord Nairne, was the third son of this third Lord Nairne and a soldier in the Government service. He had been captured by the French at the Battle of Fontenoy in 1745, which probably conveniently removed him from having to take sides during the Jacobite venture, and thereafter served in the 1st Regiment of Foot and was for some considerable time stationed in Ireland.*

In 1756 he married Brabazon Wheeler of Layrath, Co. Kilkenny and they had three children, Carolina's husband William being the second son, born in 1758.

William was of a quiet and unassuming disposition, but gregarious and a friendly man of great kindness and sympathy. That he never would know of his wife's poetic and song-writing talents does seem extraordinary but is almost certainly the case. On one occasion Carolina issued the following instructions to one of her inner circle who did know the secret: 'Do not tell Nairne lest he blab.' An anecdote in Carolina's journals says as much about her husband as it does

---

*When his military career came to an end Lt. Col. Nairne returned to Scotland and was for a time Lord Provost of St. Andrews. He died on 7 November 1782 and his wife died on 22 April 1801.

Lord Nairne, 1757-1830, Carolina's husband.

about the Gask family themselves. In 1803 the Nairnes had travelled north to Bonskeid, between the Rivers Tummel and Garry, for the christening of her eldest sister May's daughter Margaret. In 1799 May had married Dr Alexander Stewart of Bonskeid and Margaret was to be their only child. Carolina writes:

> Felt myself quite interested in Mrs. Stewart, Dr. Stewart's sister, who married a brother of Major Stewart, Fincastle (a runaway marriage), and has six children, with only a farm and [her husband] Captain Stewart's half-pay to support them. Four years having elapsed since the Doctor's marriage, and no appearance of a family, they had till now the prospect of the estate of Bonskeid; yet she showed so much unaffected goodness of heart and interest in May and the little baby, and was so pleased with her

Lady Carolina Nairne.

brother's happiness on the occasion, that I really loved her. Mr Nairne very much struck with both Captain Stewart and her being so disinterested, and said funnily, 'Well, I thought none but the Gask family could have behaved in that way.'

Edinburgh life clearly suited the Nairnes. In April 1811 Carolina's younger sister Margaret had married Alexander Keith of Ravelston in the western area of the city, and the Nairnes were frequent visitors, particularly at weekly Saturday afternoon gatherings at Ravelston House on the edge of Corstorphine Hill. Music was an integral part of these occasions and renditions by various ladies of the latest songs to come to notice were eagerly anticipated and much discussed. Interestingly, these performances were all unaccompanied as Alexander Keith and his older sister, with whom he lived before his marriage, had strong views that 'artificial' music as they termed accompaniment was intolerable. When 'The Land o' the Leal' was first performed it was generally held to have been composed by Burns on his deathbed, with the name 'Jean' substituted for 'John'. Why it had not been included in any of his printed collections led to further discussion and surmise. The composer herself was in fact at the other end of the room, had the company but known. In Carolina's own words:

> The parties could not decide why it never appeared in his [Burns] works, as his last song should have done. I never answered.

This refusal of Carolina to make public acknowledgement of her work may seem difficult to comprehend at a distance of two hundred years and from a world that ever encourages the beating of one's own drum, but there was in fact initially nothing so very unusual about it. 'The Floo'ers o' the Forest', the lament for loss at the Battle of Flodden, had been printed and published anonymously in 1746 and its authoress Jean (Jane) Elliot was not revealed until some thirty years later. Lady Anne Barnard's authorship of 'Auld Robin Gray' had also remained long a secret. For some, disguise even became something of a game; the author Clementina Stirling Graham delighted in 'personation' or 'personification' which involved appearing to friends and acquaintances in an assumed guise, much of the fun she had with it being recorded some years later by Dr John Brown in his 'Mystifications'. And indeed the 'Wizard of the North' himself, Walter Scott, had the early Waverley novels published anonymously. Scott in fact was a second cousin of Alexander Keith and he and Carolina certainly did meet at Ravelston.

It was in some ways a small world they inhabited. For instance the Oliphant family minister, Mr Erskine of Muthil, had two children who were frequently at these gatherings. One was William,

I've heard ...... of a lilting
At our ewes milking
Lasses a lilting before break of day
But now there's a moaning
On ilka green looming
Since the flowers of the forest are a wed away

At bought? in the gloamin
Nae blythe lads are roamin
'Mang stacks wi' the lasses at bogle to play
Nae laughin nae gabbin but sighing & sobbin
Ilk ane lifts her leglin & hies her away

O dool for the order—
Sent our lads to the border
The English for ance by guile gat the day
The flowers of the forest that aye shone the foremost
The pride of our land lies cauld in the clay
We'll hear nae mair lilting
At our ewes milking
The women & bairns are dowy & wae
Ilk ane sits dreary
Lamenting her dearie
Since our brave foresters are a wed away.

The Floo'ers o' the Forest in Carolina's handwriting.

Lord Kinedder, a judge and bosom pal of Walter Scott, and the other his sister Mary Ann who had married the Lord Advocate, Archibald Campbell Colquhoun. She and Carolina had been friends since childhood and it had been the loss of Mary Ann's infant daughter that had occasioned what is arguably Carolina's most poignant lyric.

But none of them except Mary Ann knew of the Gask songstress in their midst. That knowledge was reserved for a very small group of ladies consisting of Elizabeth and Agnes Hume, daughters of Lord

David Hume, Baron of Exchequer, and Helen Walker of Dalry who became the conduit for Carolina's songs reaching print. The music publisher Robert Purdie had decided to embark on a series of Scots song collections under the title of *The Scottish Minstrel* and a sort of editorial committee had formed for the purpose of sifting and selecting material to be included. It consisted of the above three ladies and Carolina herself, but all her contributions were either anonymous or signed 'B.B.' or 'Mrs. Bogan of Bogan', or sometimes 'S.M.' for 'Scottish Minstrel'. She also involved herself in a deal of text editing, thus furthering her previous intention of improving the national song, but only her three colleagues and some of her family were in on the secret; not even Purdie nor his editor Robert Smith were included. Here is an example of one of Purdie's letters to Mrs. Bogan of Bogan concerning Carolina's song 'The Mitherless Lammie':

83 Princes Street,
Monday 5th April

MADAM,
I beg leave to send you a copy of 'The Lammie,' which is just finished, my reason for sending it to you instead of Miss Corbett, as you desired, is in consequence of the accompaniment being so much altered by Mr. Dun, or indeed totally altered, the accompaniment you gave me being so very incorrect.

I also beg to enclose a note I had from Mr. Dun regarding the Title, and if it meets the Author's approbation, I should like the word children left out, as it gives the idea of something so trifling. The song is really pretty, and will be sung by grown-up people with much pleasure. Besides this, Mr. Dun says (for I have seen him this evening), that the first part is too low set for children. As he offers his name as having put the accompaniment, this will be in

*THE LAMMIE.

cou'd_na been bet_ter, But it wad gae wit_less the warld to see, The

foe that it fear'd not, it saw not it heard not, Was watching its wand'ring frae

Bon_ning_ton Lea.

O what then befell it, 'twere waefu' to tell it,
   *Tod Lowrie kens best, wi' his lang head sae sly;
He met the pet lammie, that wanted its mammie,
   And left its kind hame, the wide warld to try.
We miss't at day dawin', we miss't at night fauin';
   Its wee shed is tenantless under the tree;
Ae nicht i' the gloamin', it wad gae a roamin';
   'Twill frolic nae mair upon Bonnington Lea.

   *The Scotch word, for Fox.

63

favour of the scale, but this is only if quite agreeable to the ladies, and

> I am respectfully,
> Madam,
> Your obliged Servt.,
> Rob. Purdie.

The Mitherless Lammie

The mitherless lammie ne'er miss'd its ain mammie,
    We tentit it kindly by nicht and by day;
The bairnies made game o't, it had a blythe hame o't,
    Its food was the gowan, wi' dew drops o' May.
Without tie or fetter, it couldna' been better,
    But it wad gae witless the warld to see,
The foe that it fear'd not, it saw not, it heard not,
    Was watching its wand'ring frae Bonnington Lea.

Oh what then befell it, 'twere waefu' to tell it,
    Tod Lowrie kens best, wi' his lang heid sae sly;
He met the pet lammie, that wanted its mammie,
    And left its kind hame, the wide warld to try.
We miss'd at day dawin', we miss'd at nicht fa'in;
    Its wee shed is tenantless under the tree;
Ae nicht i' the gloamin', it wad gae a 'roamin';
    'Twill frolic nae mair upon Bonnington Lea.

Carolina was also not averse to disguising her handwriting when writing to these gentlemen whilst under the guise of 'Mrs. B. of B.' In one such letter she writes:

If Mr. Smith wishes to have the very sweet air 'Mordelia', and has not got words, perhaps the few lines enclosed may do. They were thought of long ago, when I hoped that air was considered as Scottish. If not wanted, please send me them again, as possibly they may do for some other purpose, being a bit of graphickism that I would not like quite to lose.

'Her Home She Is Leaving' is the song referred to and is a pastoral in English well-suited to the form of the melody mentioned:

The joys of the past, more faintly recalling,
Sweet visions of peace on her spirit are falling,
And the soft wing of time, as it speeds for the morrow,
Wafts a gale that is drying the dew drops of sorrow.

Carolina's friend Helen Walker seems to have been the normal discreet intermediary for her letters but when it came to presenting herself it appears that Carolina on occasion dressed herself in the guise of the said Mrs. Bogan, a lady of 'olden times', in order to visit her publisher and maintain anonymity. This does seem somewhat far-fetched, but the younger Carolina in her liveliness and impishness would certainly have been up for such a ploy, though this subterfuge was surely not undertaken for primarily light-hearted reasons. Another factor that may have been influential in Carolina's desire for anonymity was consideration for her husband and his position within society. It was perhaps not the done thing for the wife of a relatively senior member of the military establishment to be known as a songstress, and one too who glorified the other side, or so it may have seemed to her. This was obviously not a factor before their marriage, but it may have had some influence thereafter.

One thing is quite clear and that is Carolina had no thought of remuneration in any way. She was by now a quiet and dignified gentlewoman and, as she had always done, displayed the Christian virtues of modesty and self-effacement. It appears that she had previously a deep spiritual experience during the address of a visiting divine while

THE WHITE ROSE OF GASK

*Margaret Stewart of Bonskeid (Mrs Stewart Sandeman), 1803-83,
Carolina's niece.*

attending worship in Murthly Castle on some occasion in 1797. This
visiting preacher, a Mr Buckle, was described as a 'winner of souls'
and clearly Carolina's was won, though it could hardly be described
as being lost prior to this, brought up as she had been in a practising
religious household. Perhaps the secret lies in a short exchange re-
membered by her niece Margaret Stewart Sandeman, who writes:

I had as a child expressed to my dearest aunt [Carolina] the wish that the title might be restored. [The Nairne peerage had been attainted along with the forfeiture of their estates as a result of their Jacobitism.] 'Ah Maggy,' she replied, 'we should have no keen wishes concerning earthly things.'

Carolina had previously written a song on this very subject, 'The Attainted Scottish Nobles':

Oh, some will tune their mournfu' strains
To tell of hame-made sorrow,
And if they cheat you o' your tears,
They'll dry afore the morrow.
Oh, some will sing their airy dreams,
In verity they're sportin',
My sang's o' nae sic thewless themes,
But wakin', true misfortune.

Ye Scottish nobles, ane and a',
For loyalty attainted,
A nameless bardie's wae to see
Your sorrows unlamented.
For if your fathers ne'er had fought
For heirs of ancient royalty –
You're down the day that might ha'e been
At the top o' honour's tree a'.

For old hereditary right,
For conscience' sake they stoutly stood;
And for the crown their valiant sons
Themselves have shed their injured blood;
And if their fathers ne'er had fought
For heirs of ancient royalty,

They're down the day that might ha' been
At the top o' honour's tree a'.

It seems likely that this was written before her marriage and certainly the sentiments expressed did not arise from any self-interest, though they could hardly be termed forward-looking in any way. As things were to turn out, her niece's wish was in fact granted in 1824. After much lobbying, led latterly by Sir Walter Scott, the attainted titles were restored to their owners and Major William Nairne became Lord Nairne and Carolina his Baroness. It made no particular difference to their lives and one suspects made not a jot of difference to them personally either. It is worth noting that William was honoured by a Bill exclusively for himself, presented to Parliament by the Earl of Liverpool, who was Prime Minister at the time, ('by the King's command') for the restoration to him of his Grandfather's title.

One aspect of Carolina's most successful songs is the fact that they are written in Scots. One would imagine that she herself might be expected to hold strong views on this question, but in fact her sentiments are perhaps surprising. During the preparation work for the publication of the six volumes of *The Scottish Minstrel* (1821-24) there had been some feeling in the ladies' committee that only songs written in Scots should be considered for inclusion. Carolina, in a letter to Helen Walker, took the opposite viewpoint:

It never occurred to me that only Scotch words should be admitted; indeed, I think the field ought to be as large as possible, to prevent the temptation of introducing trash to fill up the volumes . . . I am not sure on what principle you are anxious to encourage the Scottish dialect, though I am far from objecting to it, because of its energy. But there is something so civilized in the English, that I prefer it in common, and I observe our servants and everybody now try to express themselves so as to avoid broad Scotch.

Examples of Carolina's handwriting.

That this was the view of someone whose success in using 'Scotch', in her own eyes at least, was already established, says as much about the mores of the day as it does about the inclinations of the writer. Edinburgh society was by this time without question looking south, despite the great literary successes of Scott and Burns in particular, and it was no accident that the great enlightenment writers and thinkers were expressing themselves solely in English. It is doubtful if David Hume, Dugald Stewart and Adam Ferguson would have achieved the same international impact they had if they had been writing purely in Scots. And indeed, Gaelic and Latin aside, it is hard to think of any non-literary work emanating from Scotland that was not written in English.

As with most creative people, Carolina wrote more than was actually published and her notebooks are full of fragments and larger pieces which did not, for whatever reason, reach the printed page. Most of them illustrate the strengths of her work and bear her own particular stamp, even though most are unfinished. 'Bonny Lass of Inchgarrow' owes more than a nod to the old Border ballads:

'Bonny lass of Inchgarrow,
Tell me your cause of sorrow,
Hide not aught and ere the morrow
Maybe I'll relieve ye.'

'When Yarrow burn wins up the hill,
When husks the hungry pleughman fill,
When morning dew-drops turn the mill,
Kind neighbour, I'll believe ye.'

'O willow, willow, wan and weeping,
O'er thy boughs the blast is sweeping,
Or lang on Death's dark pillow sleeping
I'll be low aneath ye.'

And 'Come awa' to the Hills' shows a similarity to the older ballad of 'Huntingtower' which Carolina tried her hand at as well, but in this case revealing a darker, more melancholic aspect:

'Come awa' to the hills, to the hills, to the hills,
    O come to the hills wi' me,
Come awa' to the hills, to the hills, to the hills,
    The wild deer and heath cock to see.'

O gladly, O gladly, wi' light bounding steps,
    O gladly I gaed up the hill,
An' far o'er the heather, tho' rough were the weather,
    Wad mount wi' a hearty goodwill.

'Come awa' to the hills, to the hills, to the hills,
    O I'd come to the hills wi' thee,
Come awa' to the hills, to the hills, to the hills,
    But tell me wha shall I gang wi'?'

Now sadly, O sadly, where aince ga'ed I gladly,
  Now lanely and waefu' will be,
For far are they fled, and lanely the bed
  Of ain that aince wandered wi' me.

Carolina's songs that undoubtedly come from her Edinburgh years show her at her most sympathetic. One group of people close at hand to Caroline Cottage and with whom she would have been very familiar were the fishwives of Musselburgh whose cries she immortalised in 'Caller Herrin'':

Wha'll buy my caller herrin'?
They're bonnie fish and halesome farin',
Wha'll buy my caller herrin',
New drawn frae the Forth?

When ye were sleepin' on your pillows,
Dream'd ye aught o' our puir fellows,
Darkling as they faced the billows,
A' to fill the woven willows?
Wha'll buy my caller herrin'?
They're no' brought here without brave darin';
Buy my caller herrin',
Haul'd thro' wind and rain.

Wha'll buy my caller herrin'?
Oh, ye may ca' them vulgar farin',
Wives and mothers maist despairin'
Ca' them lives o' men.

The song displays Carolina's innate sympathy with her fellow beings, a sympathy that she was able to put to practical account. She had heard that Nathaniel Gow, one of the sons of fiddler Niel Gow

CALLER HERRIN.

Air by Nath. Gow.

In MODERATE TIME.

Wha'll buy cal_ler her_ _rin'? They're bon_nie fish and hale_some fa_rin',

Wha'll buy cal_ler her_ _rin', New drawn frae the Forth? When

ye were sleep_in' on your pil_lows, Dream'd ye ought o' our puir fel_lows,

41

42

THE WHITE ROSE OF GASK

buy my cal_ler her_ _ rin'? Oh ye may ca' them vul_gar fa_ rin',

Wives and mith_ers maist de_spair_ing, Ca' them lives o' men.

When the creel o' herrin' passes,
Ladies, clad in silks and laces,
Gather in their braw pelisses,
Cast their heads and screw their faces.
   Wha'll buy caller herrin'? &c.

Caller herrin's no got lightlie,
Ye can trip the spring fu' tightlie,
Spite o' tauntin', flauntin', flingin',
Gow has set you a' a-singin'.
   Wha'll buy caller herrin'? &c.

Neebour wives, now tent my tellin',
When the bonny fish ye're sellin',
At ae word be in ye're dealin'_
Truth will stand when a' thing's failin'.
   Wha'll buy caller herrin'? &c.

43

who had been a visitor to Gask when she was younger, had been finding life extremely difficult as he sought to make a living from music in the capital. In an effort to be of assistance she had sent him the song anonymously in the hopes that he might be able to put a tune to it and perhaps make a little money for himself and his large family of eleven children. Put a tune to it he did, and what a tune, mimicking as it does the bells of the Tron Kirk, but it is not recorded if he ever discovered who the mystery benefactor was; given that he died in 1831 he probably never knew. Carolina's intermediary in this case was, as usual, Helen Walker, and her covering note to her friend ran as follows:

> If it is to be any use to Nathaniel, perhaps it should be dedicated to the Duchess of Athole.

One could not accuse Carolina of being unworldly, for she very well knew the value of patronage and the misfortunes that could beset those less fortunate than herself. Nathaniel Gow's patron was John Murray, fourth Duke of Atholl, and it did no harm to include appropriate dedications on a fairly regular basis.

Another of the songs from this time shows Carolina's ability to sympathise with those who suffered for their beliefs, even if those beliefs might not be expected to coincide precisely with her own.

Lament of the Covenanter's Widow

O weet and weary is the night,
　　Wi' soughin' wind and rain, O;
And he that was sae true tae me
　　Is on the hillside slain, O!

O that the hand that did the deed
　　Had lain me whaur he's lyin',

THE COVENANTER'S WIDOW'S LAMENT.

Slowly and with Mournful Expression.

O weet and wea _ ry is the night, Wi' sough_ing wind and rain, O; And he that was sae true to me, Is on the hill side slain, O! O that the hand that did the deed, Had laid me where he's

54

ly _ _ ing, The green turf o'er my peace_fu' head, The night winds

round me sigh _ _ ing.

mf

But I maun hear and I maun grieve,
    And I maun thole the morrow;
This heart's no made o' flesh and blood,
    It winna break wi' sorrow.
What's a' this gaudy warld to me,
    I canna bide the glare o't;
O gin it were the high decree
    That I micht see nae mair o't.

For he had taen the Covenant
    For Scotland's sake to dee, O,
Death to him was gain we ken,
    But oh! the loss to me, O.
But hush, hush, my rebellious heart,
    Tho' the deed was foully done —
Oh let me say, oh let me pray,
    Thy holy will be done!

55

The green turf o'er my peacefu' heid,
    The night winds round me sighin'.

What's a' this gaudy warld tae me?
    I canna bide the glare o't;
O gin it were the High Decree,
    That I micht see nae mair o't.

For he had ta'en the Covenant
    For Scotland's sake tae dee, O!
Death tae him was gain we ken,
    But oh! the loss tae me, O!

The Pentland Hills to the south of Edinburgh had in the latter part of the seventeenth century seen the brutal persecution of the Covenanters for their adherence to their chosen form of the Protestant religion and their refusal to accept the religious policies of Charles II and the restoration of episcopacy in Scotland. It was not lost on Carolina that one of the leading persecutors had been James Graham, Earl of Claverhouse, Viscount Dundee. Dundee, as he was generally known ('Bonnie Dundee' as immortalised in popular song by Sir Walter Scott), led the Jacobite army in the first Rising of 1689 and had perished in victory at Killiecrankie that same year.

The Pentland Hills

The pilgrim's feet here oft will tread
O'er this sequestered scene,
To mark whare Scotland's Martyrs lie
In lonely Rullion Green,
To muse o'er those who fought and fell,
All Presbyterians true,

Who held the League and Covenant,
Who waved the banner blue.

Like partridge tae the mountain driven,
Oh! lang and sairly tried.
Their cause they deemed the cause o' Heaven,
For that they liv'd and died.
Together here they met and prayed,
Ah! ne'er tae meet again;
Their windin' sheet the bluidy plaid,
Their grave lone Rullion Green.

Oh, faithless king, hast thou forgot
Who gave to thee thy crown?
Hast thou forgot thy solemn oath,
At Holyrood and Scone?*
Oh! fierce Dalziel! thy ruthless rage
Wrought langsome misery;
What Scottish he'rt could ever gi'e
A benison to thee!**

Oh, Claverhouse! fell Claverhouse!
Thou brave, but cruel, Graham.
Dark deeds like thine will last for aye,
Linked wi' thy blighted name.
Oh, Pentland Hills, sae fair and green,

*A small and ragged Covenanter force was defeated by Charles II's troops under General Tam Dalziel (Sir Thomas Dalyell of The Binns) on 28 November 1666 at Rullion Green on the west side of the Pentland Hills. 'Bluidy Tam', as he was known to the Covenanters, treated them with great cruelty.

**Charles II had previously promised to uphold the Covenant (the declaration of independent Scottish Presbyterianism) but went back on his word with the introduction of Episcopacy into Scotland.

When in the sunrise gleaming,
Or in the pensive gloamin' hour
Aneath the moonbeams streaming.

The 'faithless king' was Charles II, so this was quite a *volte-face* on the part of the Jacobite songstress. To Carolina loss was loss, no matter which side it might be on. And loss to her was to become more immediate and personal, when in 1830 her beloved husband William was to die and thereby bring to an end a rich and fulfilling chapter in her life. He had fallen gravely ill with jaundice in the previous autumn but appeared to have rallied a little, and indeed Carolina was able to write to her niece Christian Oliphant, daughter of her brother Laurence, as follows:

June 12th 1830.

I know it would make your kind heart feel to see Lord N. as he is now, feeble and emaciated beyond what you can well imagine; yet we are thankful there is no alarming symptom in the disease itself, and if it should be permitted to give way, he might in some degree pick up again, though he himself does not expect it.

Sadly he was proved correct and, falling victim to biliary trauma, he fell into a steep decline and died on 9 July.

One unexpected and noteworthy item that has come to light is contained in an excerpt from Lord Nairne's Will, that was dated 15 June 1826 and signed at Caroline Cottage. In amongst the various arrangements to be made at his death we find that £500 is to be sent to a 'natural son, William, now in the seafaring line'. The term 'natural son' in a Will means an acknowledged son born out of wedlock. There is no reference to this son to be found elsewhere, and it does seem somewhat out of character but the Will must be taken at face value and whether Carolina had any knowledge of this or not we shall never know. It is perfectly possible that she never had the wish or occasion to read her husband's Will and that the lawyers enacting it did not reveal this information to her out of delicacy, though £500 was a large sum. It is probably safe to assume that this son was born before William and Carolina were married and, if that is the case, then it certainly was not unusual for the time. It also seems highly likely that Carolina never knew of this son nor does he appear at any other point during her lifetime or thereafter.

7
'Fareweel Edinburgh'

Were I to tell your beauties a', my tale would ne'er be tauld;
Now, fareweel, Edinburgh, whar happy we ha'e been;
Fareweel, Edinburgh, Caledonia's Queen!
Prosperity to Edinburgh wi' every risin' sun,
And blessins be on Edinburgh till time his race has run.

IT IS NOT altogether clear why Carolina decided to leave Edinburgh after the death of her husband. It was long held that she did so as her son William suffered from ill-health and she was seeking a kinder climate. It was quite normal for those who could afford it to travel to other parts of Britain or the Continent in an effort to seek improvements in health, and this was a common prescription from doctors of the time and something that the Oliphant family had frequently done and were to do in the future. But this suggestion of her son William's ill-health was later to be robustly refuted by Margaret Harriet Steuart, her niece and daughter of her sister Amelia, and in time to become her executor.

'I have found several mistakes in written memoirs of my aunt,' she wrote long after Carolina's death. 'Their son was not delicate, neither was it on account of his health that he and his mother went abroad.'

She ought to have known, as she was in the house at his birth in 1808 and spent the next two years living with the Nairnes while attending school, and she kept in close touch with them thereafter. Young William was twenty-two years of age by the time of his father's death and it does seem curious that he appears as something of a blank page both up till then and afterwards. We do know that his education was in the hands of his mother until he reached the age of fifteen and after that was continued by tutors, firstly a Mr

Lady Nairne and her son William by Sir John Watson Gordon, 1823 (National Galleries of Scotland. Bequeathed by K. Oliphant 1903).

Alexander Patterson, and following him a Mr Fraser. We also know that he preferred the study of history to the theological learning that his mother had been keen for him to undertake. After this time one assumes that he remained with his mother to provide support and care in the same way as she and her siblings had done with her own father. That they were able to consider this at all indicates a revival in fortune which had certainly occurred since the time of the Nairnes' marriage. This increase in means must have been substantial, as from now on they were to embark on a somewhat peripatetic existence which must have occasioned considerable and ongoing expense, notwithstanding their simple tastes and frugality. They were assisted by a small army pension that Carolina received from her husband's military service, a life annuity of £300 awarded to Major Nairne and his lady when they were forced to give up their chambers in Holyrood Palace due to the visit of George IV, and also income from the rents from Caroline Cottage that was let on their departure.

Carolina's brother Laurence, who had become Laird of Gask on their father's death in 1792, put in hand the demolition of the 'auld hoose' of Gask, and the chapel as well, in 1801. Tastes were changing and the old house had become fairly dilapidated. Indeed when their uncle, Alexander Robertson of Strowan, ceremoniously carried the family bible out from the house just before it was demolished, the front door appears to have come away from its hinges and just missed him as it fell to the ground behind him. The final straw had been an attack one night by rats on the cradle of Laurence's son, also Laurence, while the baby was asleep. We know Carolina's thoughts on the matter, though the following appears to have been written in the 1820s during her Edinburgh years:

> The auld hoose, the auld hoose,
> Deserted tho' ye be,
> There ne'er can be a new hoose
> Will seem sae fair tae me.

The new house was much bigger and grander than the needs of Laurence's family merited, and indeed the cost of it was to prove quite a burden on his resources, all exacerbated by the fact that

Nairne House.

Britain was almost constantly at war during this period. Laurence had married Christian Robertson of Ardblair near Blairgowrie in 1795 and children followed thick and fast, eight of them in all. It was for the education of this large family that they moved to Durham in 1807, and thereafter Laurence indulged in a fair amount of continental travel. Indeed the whole family moved to Marseilles in 1816 and remained abroad for four years.

Laurence did not enjoy good mental health and it is clear that he could be prone to outbursts of physical violence, in particular towards his wife and family. This had led to him spending a period of time in an institution at Saughtonhall in Edinburgh prior to 1807 and much concern among his family, particularly Dr Alexander Stewart, his brother-in-law and physician. This may well have been the underlying reason for the family's travels abroad and the fact that they did not spend much time at Gask. Their absence did not do the estate any favours and does seem curious when the new house was not long completed. It rather confirms the likely seriousness of Laurence's con-

dition. He died in 1819 in Paris and is buried in Père Lachaise ceme-
tery, and his eldest son Laurence died in 1824. His second son James
then became Laird but remained single till 1840, when he married his
cousin Henrietta Gillespie Graham of Orchill. Carolina's two older
sisters had also both died, Amelia in 1808 and May in 1819.

So in 1830 when Carolina's husband William died a return to
Gask was probably not a considered option for her and her son.
Carolina was broken-hearted by her bereavement, for she had, in her
own words, been 'a too happy wife and mother', and the loss of her
husband clearly marks a change in her life and her demeanour. One
could almost say that the sparkle went out of her eyes, and her mind
dwelt increasingly more on spiritual matters. Caroline Cottage must
have seemed an empty shell, constantly reminding her of happier
times and dominated by the shadow of her much-loved husband.
The last entry in her Journal from there is dated 'August 1830':

> With a heavy but I trust resigned heart have tied up these
> papers preparatory to leaving this once happy home – long
> happy and with deep gratitude to the giver of all good, felt
> and acknowledged to be so thro his unmerited love. May
> His Presence go with us, the widow and only child of one
> now I trust rejoicing among the redeemed – and O may
> we be safely and mercifully led thro all the trials of time to
> a happy immortality for his sake who has done all for us
> sinful creatures.

She and her son William first travelled to Clifton near Bristol
to be with her niece Margaret, her brother Laurence's daughter, who
had recently married Thomas Kington of Charlton House, Shepton
Mallet, Somerset. Margaret and her sisters had taken up residence in
the area for health reasons, which is perhaps how the match had come
about. The youngest of these sisters was also named Caroline and she
too had poetry in her blood, albeit in English rather than Scots. But

William, Lord Nairne, 1808-37, Carolina's son.

she did not enjoy robust health either and was to fall ill of an undisclosed ailment; she died on 9 February 1831. It is a mark of the times that this Caroline had already lost her parents, her elder brother and three of her sisters within the space of the previous eleven years.

Yet another death in her close family may well have been the trigger for Carolina and William to move on, and this they did in July of 1831, when they travelled to Ireland, to Kingstown on the edge of Dublin and from there south to Enniskerry in County Wicklow. Carolina's husband had been born in Drogheda in County Louth in 1758, where his father had been on military station, and Carolina had long wanted to visit Ireland for this reason. A short excerpt from a letter she wrote to her friend Helen Walker back in Edinburgh perhaps suggests a somewhat protective attitude towards her son which would go some way to explain his apparent lack of independent activity. She writes:

> William, like all boys, is fond of riding, so I got a pony for him, and he often went to the post, and came back with letters, all safe and sound.

William was at this stage twenty-three years old. It is perhaps not entirely relevant but worth noting that Horatio Nelson had by the same age achieved the rank of Post Captain in the Royal Navy, with victories already to his name and three ships of the line under his command. Nelson was obviously exceptional, but William's lack of independent action does seem curious, given that both his father and grandfather had been serving soldiers, and contacts and preferment were readily available to him. It is clear however that his duty to his mother that included being by her side was a paramount concern for him, and should be counted greatly to his credit.

Mother and son were clearly well-liked in Ireland, as reflected in the remarks some forty years later of Abraham Williams, then an old man who had lived opposite the Nairnes at this time:

> Well I knew Lady Nairne indeed, and she was as much of a leddy as any I ever knowed. And young Lord Nairne . . . he

was very thin, very thin and delicate, but a fine and gentle young man . . . She was a fine lady, tall and stately, fine nose and features, and so simple. Her servants spoke of her with great kindness.

While at Enniskerry Carolina's muse was not silent. She was already familiar with Irish music and song and she had read and admired the works of Thomas Moore, though she did feel strongly that, like Burns, his verse sometimes strayed from the paths of purity.

> Sweet poet! be true to thy lofty inspiring;
> While, bound by thy magic, the skies half unfurled,
> Youth, beauty, and taste are with rapture admiring,
> O spread not around them the fumes of this world.
> ('A Heavenly Muse')

Another result of her stay in Ireland was the admiration she was to develop for the 'Irish peasantry' as they were quaintly termed. However she was not impressed with their spiritual state and it was to occasion the following song:

> Wake, Irishmen, wake, let your slumbers be over,
> Our children will look to our day when we're gone,
> The clouds and thick darkness, now o'er us may hover,
> The sun will yet shine on fair Erin!
>
> Strong is the arm that is stretched out to save us,
> High is the rock where our confidence rests,
> It is not in man, with his worst threats to brave us.
> Then Irishmen, wake, let your slumbers be over,
> Our children will look to our day when we're gone,

Tho' clouds and thick darkness now o'er us may hover,
The sun will yet shine on fair Erin!

It could be thought that this first verse was a nationalist call to arms to rid Ireland of the oppressive Hanoverian yoke, but it is very clear that Carolina was never a political being and the second and third verses are to reveal her true meaning:

We love you as men, and as brothers we love you,
Our hearts long to free you from Popery's hard chain;
For the sake of your undying souls, we would move you,
To know the true friends of fair Erin.
Come better, come worse, we will never surrender,
For the cause that our forefathers stood, we will stand;
To the last drop of blood, our own Isle we'll defend her.
Then Irishmen, rise! Let your slumbers be over;
Our children will look to our day when we're gone,
Tho' clouds and thick darkness now o'er us may hover,
The sun will yet shine on fair Erin!

It is not likely this would have won her many friends in Ireland outwith her own Protestant circle and it displays a side to her that has not shown itself hitherto. However it was almost certainly never performed during their stay, and in 1834 Carolina and her son set off on their travels around continental Europe. They were accompanied by Carolina's sister Margaret, Lady Keith, who had been widowed some fifteen years earlier, and their niece Margaret Harriet Steuart of Dalguise, the daughter of their sister Amelia.

It seems a curious and unsettled life they now embarked upon, visiting Paris, Florence, Rome, Naples, Geneva, Interlaken, Baden, and then Mannheim for the winter of 1835, where Lady Keith and Harriet Steuart left them and returned home. Carolina paints a picture from Mannheim in a letter to her niece, Margaret Stewart Sandeman:

27th February 1836

Our winter's residence here has not been altogether as satisfactory as I had hoped. My great attraction was in an excellent clergyman, who was able to officiate only twice after we came. Here there are many English families, and what is called very genteel society. There is also the court of the Grand Duchess Dowager of Baden, a niece-in-law of poor Josephine, and adopted daughter of Napoleon. You will scarcely believe what a fuss the English make about this French lady; she goes to their balls and musical parties, and being now a Royal Highness, is treated something like a queen by them. She was very handsome and is said to be very accomplished. Her only unmarried daughter is, I believe, really a fine girl of nineteen.* I have not seen either, as I do nothing, as usual, beyond morning calls on a few acquaintances. I say with thankfulness that I have been better on the Continent than for a long time in our humid islands; yet age must tell, however gently.

In the spring of 1836 they travelled to Baden-Baden. 'This is a delightful spot', wrote Carolina. 'Nairne's taste for wild nature at least equals mine.'

Then they moved on to Berlin, where in 1837 they were rejoined by Lady Keith and Harriet Steuart, and it was there that William caught the cold that soon became severe influenza, which

*This lady, Princess Marie of Baden, was rather surprisingly to become the Duchess of Hamilton. In 1843 she married William Hamilton who in 1852 became 11th Duke of Hamilton. They lived mainly in Paris and Baden.

was epidemic in that area at the time. A return to Britain was decided on in aid of his deteriorating health, but the travellers only managed to reach Brussels where, on 7 December, in a house in the Rue de Louvain, he died.

'I have not a single regret about William's upbringing,' Carolina wrote to a niece. 'He was trained for the Kingdom, whither he has gone.' And there follow remarks that indicate what changes had taken place in Carolina's own character over the previous thirty years. 'I was laughed at for not having him taught dancing; but I knew its snares too well. What else does the Bible lead us to expect when it says – "Therefore the world knoweth us not, because it knew him not." Yet there never was a merrier home than ours. Your Uncle was full of fun, and kept his best spirits for his own home.'

'My dear aunt has suffered much,' wrote her niece Margaret Stewart Sandeman who arrived in Brussels with her own daughter Margaret on the very day of William's funeral, and just too late to be present. 'Yet,' she continues, 'she has seen mercy in every step, softening the anguish of this heavy trial.' She goes on to describe her aunt at that time:

> It was a cold December night. The north wind, more dry and sifting than in Britain, was felt in the large apartment in spite of the open stove and the screen that surrounded her sofa. Lady Nairne sat at a writing-table. The green shade of the lamp concealed in a great measure the wrinkled face and blood-shot eyes; and she looked still lovely, and much younger in her seventy-second year than one would have expected. Her cap, of Queen Mary shape, had a large white crape handkerchief thrown over it. She made the kindest and most minute inquiries about everything at home, and when the effort became too great, she gave me a book to read.

Two further letters from Carolina to Margaret Sandeman give an insight into her own state of mind after this latest bereavement. Later in December 1837 she writes:

Though writing, even to friends, is no longer, as formerly, one of my occupations, I cannot resist the temptation now offered of thanking you for your kind letter, and sympathy with me under the heavy affliction which it pleased our Heavenly Father to send me. No one but myself can know what I have lost in my darling companion of almost thirty years, as none besides could witness his never-ceasing tenderness and confidence. Whilst I had him, the thought that it was a thing possible that I might lose him, would at times embitter to me our delightful intercourse. This, I know now, arose from excess of attachment and surely I have much, much reason to give thanks for the grace that enabled me to resign him at last with the full conviction that all was well for him and me. You are the first to whom I have written of my inmost feelings, as I really have not strength of mind or body for much.

Then later, on 9 November 1839, she writes from Nice:

I do indeed very rarely write to any one; but I must, with my own hand and heart, thank you my long-loved Margaret, for your kind and satisfactory letter. I am much weakened in mind and body since I saw you last, and how can it be otherwise? Age and sorrow will tell, yet I am here a monument of mercy and tender dealing. Surely loving-kindness and mercy have followed me all the days of my life, and I know will follow me to the end. I have often in other days felt a chill of apprehension when I read the words, 'He that loveth son or daughter more than Me is not worthy of Me.' You are aware of the danger. My mother, when she had six thriving infants, resigned them every night into our Saviour's hands; she learned much by the death of her first lovely boy at a year old, and was six years without a child. Then your mother came to be her comfort. Adieu dearest M. May you and I, with all we love, meet in due time to part no more, and in the meantime may you be enabled to fulfil your mission.

From here onwards a deep sadness and resignation descended on Carolina, though borne with her customary fortitude and Christian hope. She continued travelling for the next two years in the company of her grand-niece Margaret Fraser Sandeman (Barbour), grand-daughter of her eldest sister May. They visited Munich, Nice, Pau and Salzburg, and the spring of 1842 found them back in Paris.

For all her protestations though not complaints of weakness, Carolina seems to have enjoyed reasonable health at this time. Indeed tinnitus seems to have been the only drawback – 'It is as if all the bees in the country had assembled in my ears,' she wrote.

Back at Gask, Carolina's nephew James Oliphant, who had married his cousin Henrietta Gillespie Graham of Orchill in 1840, had for some time been generously endeavouring to persuade his aunt to return to the family home in her old age. She had been resisting this for fear of being an encumbrance on James and his wife, but eventually, after entreaties from both of them, Carolina gave way and James and Henrietta travelled out to Paris in 1843 and escorted her back to Gask.

8

'This Warld's Cares Are Vain'

Gask, 17th August, 1843

Resolved as I was but lately never again to visit Scotland, here I am, by the kind persuasion of my nephew Oliphant and his amiable Lady. We arrived the 7th of last month after a prosperous journey and voyage, for which I fancied myself quite unfit in my feeble state.

Thus wrote Carolina on her return to 'this sweet place' after so long an interval. And she continues:

I hope I am in the path of duty. I do not see what use I am of in this world . . . Everything leads me back to early youth, and what has passed between my first and last abode at Gask seems as a mixed and wonderful dream.

But she soon recovered her normal interest in things around her and in particular those of a spiritual nature, as she shows in this letter to her Edinburgh friend of *Scottish Minstrel* days, Helen Walker:

I do hope and trust with you that the commotions in the Church of Scotland may tend to the advancement of the Gospel in its purity.* I am anxious for the prosperity of

---

*The established Church of Scotland split into two in 1843 over the question of State and lay intervention through patronage in the appointment of ministers. This was the culmination of a long-running and bitter dispute. The breakaway Free Church held that only the Church should exercise this authority and this 'Disruption', as it became known, had a huge effect on Scottish religious and civil life, both at the time and thereafter.

the Free Church . . . the true disciples will be kept in peace and safety I have no doubt.'

Though a staunch Episcopalian all her life, her generous sympathies went out to the outcast ministers of the Church of Scotland who made great sacrifices for their principles. Her contribution to the Sustentation Fund of the new Free Church was typical of her, sending much of her silver to her great-niece, Margaret Fraser Sandeman, with the following instruction:

> the old forks, spoons, etc. which I shall now no more require, take them to any silversmith who will give the value for old silver. It will be just as well if they are melted, as they have the crest. Of course you will not say where they come from.

Ever since her wedding Carolina had been a regular supporter of charities of all kinds. Her gifts were always anonymous and they appear to have continued with even more regularity at this time. Dr Thomas Chalmers, a central figure in these Church of Scotland commotions and leader of the breakaway Free Church, was able to reveal shortly after her death that the recent and anonymous gift of £300 towards the cost of the work he was leading amongst the destitute of Edinburgh's West Port had in fact been given by 'a lady of another denomination, Lady Nairne of Perthshire'. He continued:

> It enabled us to purchase sites for schools and a church, and we have got a site in the very heart of the locality with a very considerable extent of ground for a washing-green, a washing-house, and a play-ground for children.

At that time one quarter of the population of the West Port were paupers on the poor-roll, and a further quarter were street beggars, thieves or prostitutes. £300 was a considerable sum in those days and Chalmers had been under strict instructions from Carolina that her identity was not to be revealed. Now he was able to mention further donations that she had made to charitable work in the city and beyond, £50 towards Gaelic schools in the Highlands being one such sum.

Her gifts of this nature were numerous, nor shall the quantity and amounts ever be fully known. Throughout her travels too she had been in the habit of making gifts to needy causes and there are records of officials in various European cities and towns in which she stayed later recording their thanks and appreciation for the generosity of the Scottish lady in their midst. Aside from her travels she spent nothing on herself, and her philanthropy is summed up in a letter of 1844 to Helen Walker:

> I wish to know if you have any object in view, that is connected with the advancement of religion, and that a few spare pounds would assist. I often think of the Jews, and would not lose sight of them. I will desire Mr. Lindsay to give you £25, and I am sure it will be judiciously employed in the great cause. I will not make apologies for giving you this trouble.
>
> N.B. The above is one of our secrets.

Now back home at Gask, Carolina's health was to deteriorate. She was partially paralysed by a small stroke in December 1843, but was able to recover and though remaining fairly weak thereafter, did manage one further visit to Edinburgh in 1844. During this visit she was in the house of a friend when a young lady in the company offered to entertain with a song and made the innocent remark 'I am very fond of this air, and I am sure you will like it,' and proceeded to play and sing 'The Land o' the Leal.' Characteristically its author made no acknowledgement of previous acquaintance with the song.

Interior of the new chapel at Gask.

'Life is a perpetual repetition of resignation and submission,' wrote Carolina in 1845. 'I hope it will soon be over.'

And over it was soon to be. With the expense being borne jointly by herself and her nephew James a new chapel for Episcopalian worship was being built at Gask on the site of the old parish church and on Saturday 25 October of that year Carolina was brought in a wheelchair to see it as it neared completion. 'The place will soon be ready for me,' she remarked, and she was right, for two days later, aged seventy-nine, she peacefully reached her 'lang hame'. She was buried in the New Chapel and much later a granite cross was erected nearby in her memory. Above her name it carries the Latin inscription 'Carmina Morte Carente' ('Her songs lack death').

Many years before, in 1819, while attending her dying sister May at Bonskeid, she had knelt by the invalid's bed and seemed to see a radiance around her sister who had apparently said 'I could shout for joy!'. 'Ask me no questions,' Carolina would say in later

The memorial cross to Lady Nairne at Gask.

years, 'about the visible glory that seemed to encircle my beloved sister in that solemn hour.' It matters not whether this was in fact or in mind. It displays the certainty that Carolina shared with all her family.

In her final time at Gask Carolina had been asked if her songs could be put together in a single publication, and to this she had consented, albeit with one predictable stricture. There was to be no mention of the name of the author. It is not clear who was the instigator of this project. Robert Purdie's music and publishing business at 83 Princes Street in Edinburgh had by this time been taken over by his son John. Like Purdie senior, Robert Smith, the original editor of *The Scottish Minstrel*, was dead by this time, but the music arranger Finlay Dun was to oversee this new publication. It seems likely that Helen Walker was the driving force behind the collection and indeed Carolina had already sent her some unpublished work for inclusion,

NEW EDITION.

Lays of Strathearn,

BY

CAROLINE BARONESS NAIRNE

the

SYMPHONIES & ACCOMPANIMENTS

By the late

FINLAY DUN.

PATERSON & SONS

27, GEORGE STREET, EDINBURGH.   152, BUCHANAN STREET, GLASGOW.

17, PRINCES STREET, PERTH, & 36, NEWMARKET STREET, AYR.

LONDON, HUTCHINGS & ROMER, 9, CONDUIT STREET, REGENT STREET. W.

Title page of an early edition of The Lays of Strathearn.

but Carolina's death was to occur while the book was being put together. It was then that application was made to Lady Keith, her sole surviving sister, to see if permission might be granted to publish the collection and include the author's name. Here is Margaret Keith's reply:

> January 16th 1846,
>
> My niece [Margaret Stewart Sandeman] and I are both of opinion that my beloved sister Nairne had not the least thought or wish to have her name ever published as authoress of those beautiful words to different tunes; yet we think there can be nothing wrong in letting it be known that she wrote them.

The collection *Lays of Strathearn* was duly published that year and the first edition sold out in a matter of weeks. It was to become a staple of Scots song for the remaining fifty years of the century. Margaret Keith was to die the following year, and the world is greatly in her debt for allowing errors and misinterpretations to be corrected and for throwing a gentle spotlight on her most gifted sister.

Carolina's final song, written when she was seventy-six in 1842 and set to the Irish air 'Eileen Aroon', had been one of yearning for what had now come to pass:

> Would you be young again?
>   So would not I –
> One tear to mem'ry given,
>   Onward I'd hie.
> Life's dark flood forded o'er,
> All but at rest on shore,
> Say, would you plunge once more,
>   With home so nigh?

WOULD YE BE YOUNG AGAIN.

Air—Ailen Aroon.

SLOWLY. *mf* *p*

young a — gain? So would not I—

cres.

One tear to mem' — ry giv'n, On — ward I'd hie.

cres.

cres.

Life's dark flood ford — ed o'er All but at

mf

44

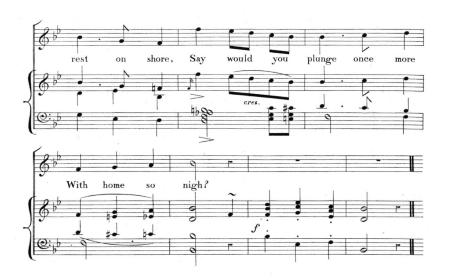

rest on shore, Say would you plunge once more

With home so nigh?

If you might, would you now
    Tread o'er your way?
Wander thro' stormy wilds,
    Faint and astray?
Night's gloomy watches fled,
Morning all beaming red,
Hope's smiles around us shed,
    Heav'nward __ away.

Where there are those dear ones,
    Our joy and delight __
Dear and more dear, tho' now
    Hidden from sight.
Where they rejoice to be,
There is the land for me;
Fly time, fly speedily,
    Come life and light.

45

If you might, would you now
    Retrace your way?
Wander through thorny wilds,
    Faint and astray?
Night's gloomy watches fled,
Morning all beaming red,
Hope's smiles around us shed,
    Heavenward – away.

Where are they gone, of yore
    My best delight?
Dear and more dear, tho' now
    Hidden from sight.
Where they rejoice to be,
There is the land for me,
Fly time, fly speedily;
    Come life and light!

9
'And Joy for aye Be wi' Us A"

CAROLINA OLIPHANT was clearly loved by all. Whether it be in her early days of childhood, in the vitality of her youth, in her serene married life, and finally in the latter years, she inspired affection amongst those she mingled with. Thomas Kington Oliphant, himself a later Laird and chronicler of Gask, was able to report as follows:

> In 1868 I spoke with her old maid, Henriette Vouaillat, at Geneva. After listening to a long catalogue of Lady Nairne's virtues, I asked, 'But had your mistress no faults? You are describing a perfect character.' 'Sir,' said the old Genovese, 'my mistress came as near to an angel as the weakness of human nature would allow. The only thing amiss I could see in her was that she disliked my marrying or otherwise leaving her.'

> Carolina's grand-niece, Margaret Fraser Sandeman (Barbour), who travelled with her in her latter years, had the opportunity of getting to know her at that time: 'Poetry burned in her soul higher than any flame but faith,' she wrote, 'and she was always trying how to send home a divine truth on the wing of a fine thought.'

> After describing the shock of arriving in Brussels to find that her cousin William Nairne, Carolina's son, had died and been buried on that very day, she continues:

> Lady Nairne sat at a writing table, and she looked still lovely, and much younger in her seventy-second year than we would have expected.

> One evening, while reading aloud to her, we came upon a note discussing the authorship of 'The Land o' the

Margaret Fraser Sandeman (Barbour), 1823-92, painted in 1874 by Norman Macbeth.

Leal'. To the young reader it was somewhat like going to the cannon's mouth to read it to her, and if blushes could betray the knowledge of a secret, Lady Nairne's observant eye must have seen them.

I never saw her allow herself (at this time) to laugh heartily but once, and it was not long after our first meeting (some years earlier). She had been repeating some lines of which she said she had often tried to discover the author. On my insisting that his name was in a collection of poetry, she said 'You must bring it to me next night.' She did not forget, and I told her the name of the author was 'Anonymous'. When a very little child I had got it into my mind that this was a clever man who wrote most of the pretty things we learned. The error had not been discovered and the existence of 'Anon' was firmly believed in. To have made such a blunder before most people would have been a lasting humiliation, but not with her. She was kinder than ever and said:

'Now tell me dear Maggy where do you learn your hymns when at Springland?'

'On a crooked little beech tree, just like an arm-chair, after breakfast till church time on Sundays.'

'And at Bonskeid, which is the favourite seat?'

'Up in the west wood where you painted the house from.'

'I hope they do not oblige you to write verses of your own, as some are made to do.'

'No.'

'And you never tried?'

'Never.'

'True poetry is involuntary; it will force its own way. You and I must have many talks about these wonderful men, Anonymous and Anon, who have between them caused me more delight than many authors.

I must tell you a story of our youth at Gask, where the mistake of a word not only caused merriment for us at the time, but ever since. Aunt Harriet had got a special summons on horseback to Athole to go to see Lady Lude who was said to be so ill that if she wished to see her in life she must come instantly.* Aunt Harriet gave a letter ordering a large chaise [coach] to the horseman to deliver in Perth on his arrival there, nine miles distant as you know. We all set to making preparations for her journey. May, your grandmother, was the director, as in everything else, and we were all seated around Aunt Harriet in her grief, wondering how the 'chaise' she had ordered (she had written to Perth that the biggest to be had should be sent immediately) was so long in coming, as the journey to Blair Atholl was tedious and it was getting late. Suddenly the door of the room opened, and two men entered carrying an enormous cheese! Aunt Harriet was always a great laugher, but this time owing to the tension on the nerves caused by sorrowful preparations, parting with us, and the illness of her sister, she was seized with an immoderate fit. Tears even ran down, the more her ludicrous mistake in spelling became plain to her. She without power to explain, the two men with the cheese on the floor between them, we gazing in utter and uncomprehending wonder, formed a scene we could never forget. The journey was given up till next morning.

Another niece was Margaret Harriet Steuart, daughter of Carolina's sister Amelia. Harriet had been Carolina's Executor** and had gone to South Africa where her brother John was High Sheriff (Chief Justice) of the Cape of Good Hope.

*Lady Lude was Harriet's sister Charlotte Robertson, wife of John Robertson of Lude, and renowned for bullying her tenants into joining the Jacobite army in 1745.

**As well as being Carolina's Executor, Harriet Steuart was the main beneficiary of her aunt's will and the total estate amounted to something over £3800. This figure included rents from Caroline Cottage in Edinburgh, but no mention is made of the property itself. The will had originally been drawn up on 19 November 1838 in Munich.

Writing in 1894 aged ninety-seven, when she was still painting, embroidering, and playing music, she was able to remember hearing of Trafalgar and Waterloo and of entertaining Sir Walter Scott with her music, and of how she and the great novelist's daughter Sophia would 'shut the shutters that we might tell one another ghost stories in the dark'. She continues:

My earliest recollections of my Aunt Nairne are of spending a winter with her in Montrose when I was about 7 years old [1804]. She was very fond of children and in the evenings my eldest brother John and I were always allowed by her to cut out paper, paste, paint, or make any mess we pleased. My mother and I then paid a short visit to her in Portobello when they made the purchase of Caroline Cottage, now I am told called Nairne Lodge. Major Nairne, as well as his lady, was always extremely kind to me. She called me 'Quiet Maggie' as I was rather shy in those days. In June 1808 my cousin William [their son] was born in Hope Street, Edinburgh, my aunt Margaret [Oliphant] and I being then in the house. The next winter was spent by the Nairnes at 43 Queen Street, Edinburgh and I lived with them for two years, going daily to school. In July 1813 I accompanied them in a cutter bound for the Shetland Isles. To them I went, but poor Aunt Nairne was so ill at sea that we had to lay to at Peterhead whilst she and her boy were put ashore, and they both went to St. Andrews by land where they joined her sister, my Aunt Stewart of Bonskeid. My next visit to Aunt Nairne was at Holyrood House, where her husband had the royal apartments for some years, until His Majesty George IV thought fit to show himself in Scotland. It was a very pleasant dwelling; the side of the square was gloomy, but the windows of the living rooms all looked to the Park and Arthur's Seat. The chambers were

Harriet Steuart of Dalguise, 1797-1896, by R. McInnes in 1829.

of a very large size, except two smaller ones which were divided off by high screens. These were hung with very fine old tapestry, whereon were depicted immense human forms with the heads of toads. One anteroom was so very spacious that it was divided off into several, and allotted to the servants. The whole royal apartments were done up and beautified for the King, and to the very great amusement of my young cousin the throne was placed exactly where the cook's bed had stood! In 1830 Lord Nairne, whose forfeited title had been restored, died at Caroline Cottage. In 1834 we all went to Italy and spent the greater part of the winter in Rome. My aunt Keith and I came home in 1835 but we joined them in the autumn of the following year at Berlin where my poor cousin caught the cold which proved fatal in December 1837. I have found several mistakes in written memoirs of my aunt. Their son was not delicate, neither was it on account of his health that he and his mother went abroad. The cold caught at Berlin was the beginning of his illness. I was with my aunt later on at Pau and Eaux-Chaudes, and after this we were in the Pyrenees again at Biarritz and then Paris. It was to that city, in the spring of 1843, that James Oliphant came and took my aunt home to Gask, as you know, to die.

Carolina was certainly anticipating this final journey when she penned the following lines:

> The best o' joys maun ha'e an end,
>   The best o' friends maun part, I trow;
> The langest day will wear away,
>   And I maun bid fareweel tae you.
> The tear will tell when he'rts are fu';
>   For words, gin they ha'e sense ava',
> They're broken, faltering, and few;
>   Gude nicht, and joy be wi' you a'.

GUDE NICHT AND JOY BE WI' YE A'*

In
MODERATE
TIME.

mf

p

The best o' joys maun hae an end The best o' friends maun part I trow; The lang_est day will wear a_way, And I maun bid fare_weel to you. The tear will tell when hearts are fu', For words, gin they hae

*Generally played at the breaking up of a party.

52

sense a _ va, They're bro_ken, fal_ter_ing and few_Gude nicht and

joy be wi' you a'.

O we hae wandered far and wide,
  O'er Scotia's lands o' firth and fell,
And mony a simple flower we've pu'd,.
  And twined it wi' the heather bell:
We've ranged the dingle and the dell,
  The cot-house and the baron's ha';
Now we maun tak a last farewell,
  Gude nicht and joy be wi' you a'.

My harp fareweel, thy strains are past,
  Of gleefu' mirth, and heartfelt wae;
The voice of song maun cease at last,
  And minstrelsy itsel' decay.
But, oh, whar sorrow canna win,
  Nor parting tears are shed ava,
May we meet neighbour, kith and kin
  And joy for aye be wi' us a'.

53

O we ha'e wandered far and wide,
  O' Scotia's lands o' firth and fell,
And mony a simple flower we've pu'd,
  And twined it wi' the heather bell.
We've ranged the dingle and the dell,
  The cot-house and the baron's ha';
Now we maun tak' a last farewell,
  Gude nicht, and joy be wi' you a'.

My harp, fareweel, thy strains are past,
  Of gleefu' mirth, and heartfelt wae;
The voice of song maun cease at last,
  And minstrelsy itsel' decay.
But, oh! whare sorrow canna win,
  Nor parting tears are shed ava',
May we meet neighbour, kith and kin,
  And joy for aye be wi' us a'.*

It fell to an Oliphant of a later time to pen a suitable epitaph for Carolina. Writing in 1910, Ethel Maxtone-Graham (née Blair Oliphant) paid her warm tribute.

The story of her life is a story of consistent effort towards all things that are pure. Yet her nature was a dual nature – on the one side the mind was that of a woman cast in a deeply religious but narrow mould, which though great in generous charities of act and judgment, and wide in sympathies, spent itself in furthering, by every gentle and unobtrusive method possible, the mild evangelical aims of those whose views coincided with her own. Her other

*The air of the same name for this song was well-known. Others wrote lyrics to it as well, in particular Alexander Boswell (1775-1822). It is based on the Border ballad 'Armstrong's Goodnight'.

personality, that of the God-gifted poetess singing from the depths of uncontrollable inspiration, is what is left to her country and her race. Strongest in her youth and prime, this greater personality faded gradually away under the weight of her years and her griefs. But in both lives there never was a time when she was not most steadfast to the light, and most true to her trust. All the enthusiasms, the proud loyalties, the young passionate sympathies that once lit her soul, centred at last in a complete holiness of faith.

No estimate of her literary work is needed now. She wrote little, and the best of what she wrote takes a place in the foremost rank of letters, among the achievements that for ever must remain beautiful, new, and appealing. Her voice has survived the fluctuations of taste and feeling in the public mind for a hundred years, and has never suffered eclipse. For a hundred years the voices of her country people have sung 'The Land o' the Leal' and 'Caller Herrin'. Generations yet to come will sing them still. They belong to the heart of humanity.

These words still carry the same resonance and truth today.

10
'The Land o' the Leal'

I'm wearin' awa', John,
Like snow when it's thaw, John,
I'm wearin' awa'
   To the land o' the leal.
There's nae sorrow there, John,
There's neither cauld nor care, John,
The day is aye fair
   In the land o' the leal.

ONE WOULD think that the above lines had been written by someone towards the end of their days, but in fact they came from Carolina's pen while she was still in her early thirties in 1798. They were written for her friend Mary Ann Erskine, daughter of the Rev. William Erskine of Muthill, who had been the family minister at Gask. Mary Ann had married Archibald Campbell Colquhoun, Sheriff of Perthshire and then Lord Advocate and Lord Clerk Register. The Campbell Colquhouns' daughter Helen had died six days before her first birthday in 1797 and her mother was distraught. On hearing of their loss Carolina had written a letter of sympathy to her friend and with the letter had included the verses of 'The Land o' the Leal'.

Our bonnie bairn's there, John,
She was baith gude and fair, John,
And oh! we grudged her sair
   To the land o' the leal.
But sorrow's sel' wears past, John,
And joy's a-comin' fast, John,
The joy that's aye to last
   In the land o' the leal.

Mary Ann Campbell Colquhoun, 1773-1833.

With her Christian upbringing Mrs Campbell Colquhoun would have well understood the inferences in Carolina's lines, and the following verse, though added some years later, would have strongly resonated with her:

> Sae dear that joy was bought, John,
> Sae free the battle fought, John,
> That sinfu' man e'er brought
>   To the land o' the leal.
> Oh! dry your glist'ning e'e, John,
> My saul langs to be free, John,
> And angels beckon me
>   To the land o' the leal.

In the words of the folksinger Jean Redpath, this song 'is a fitting hymn for Lady Nairne herself. It certainly is where her simplicity

I'm wearin' awa John
Like snaw when its thaw John
I'm wearin' awa to the land o the leal

There's nae sorrow there John
There's neither cauld nor care John
The day's aye fair in the land of the leal
Our bonny bairn's there John
She was baith gude & fair John
And O we grudged her sair
To the land o the leal
But sorrow's sel' wears past John
And joy is comin fast John
The joy that's aye to last
In the land o the leal.
Now haud ye hal & tine John
Your day it's weel near thro John
And I'll welcome you
To the land o the leal

O dry your glistenin ee John
My soul langs to be free John
And angels beckon me
To the land o the leal.
Now fare ye weel my ain John
This world's cares are vain John
We'll meet & we'll be fain
In the land o the leal——

The Land o' the Leal in Carolina's handwriting.

and poignancy lay tightest hold of the national heart.' In Carolina's own words:

> 'The Land o' the Leal' is a happy rest for the mind in this dark pilgrimage . . . O yes! I was young then. I wrote it merely because I liked the air so much and I put these words to it.

The air in question was 'Hey tutti tatti', one of the oldest of Scots melodies and said to have been played in martial style at the Battle of Bannockburn in 1314.

Carolina was not unusual in seeking to write songs and verses in a form of vernacular Scots, and the number of female writers who were her contemporaries in this is significant. Like her, most came from privileged backgrounds and many had been enthused by Burns. But Burns himself might not have appeared if the door hadn't already been partially opened. Mention has been made of Jean Elliot's 'Floo'ers o' the Forest' being anonymously published in 1746, and later there was another version by Alison Cockburn (Rutherford); others who spring to mind are Lady Anne Lindsay (Barnard) with 'Auld Robin Gray', Joanna Baillie's 'Woo'd an Married an' a'', Lady John Scott's 'Annie Laurie', Susanna Blamire's 'And Ye Shall Walk in Silk Attire', Mary M. Campbell's 'The March of the Cameron Men', Grace Campbell's 'Jessie's Dream', Elizabeth Grant's 'Roy's Wife of Aldivalloch', Elizabeth Hamilton's 'My Ain Fireside', and from an earlier time as she died twenty years before Carolina was born, Lady Grizel Baillie's 'And Werena My Heart Licht I Wad Dee'. Other contemporary female songwriters who did not have the benefit of a privileged background would include Jean Adam ('There's Nae Luck about the Hoose'), Isobel (Tibby) Pagan ('Ca' the Yowes tae the Knowes'), and Jean Glover ('O'er the Moor amang the Heather').

THE LAND O' THE LEAL.

Air—Hey tutti taiti.

Slow, and with Tender Feeling

I'm wear_in' a_wa, John, Like snaw wreathes in thaw, John, I'm wear_in' a_wa' To the land o' the leal. There's nae sor_row there, John, There's nei_ther cauld nor care, John, The

24

day's aye fair I' the land o' the leal.

Our bonnie bairn's there, John,
She was baith gude and fair, John;
And oh! we grudg'd her sair
    To the land o' the leal.
But sorrow's sel wears past, John,
And joy's a comin' fast, John,
The joy that's aye to last
    In the land o' the leal.

Sae dear's that joy was bought, John,
Sae free the battle fought, John,
That sinfu' man e'er brought
    To the land o' the leal.
Oh! dry your glist'ning e'e, John,
My saul langs to be free, John,
And angels beckon me
    To the land o' the leal.

Oh! haud ye leal and true, John,
Your day it's wearin' thro', John,
And I'll welcome you
    To the land o' the leal.
Now fare ye weel my ain John,
This warld's cares are vain, John,
We'll meet, and we'll be fain,
    In the land o' the leal.

25

Of course there were other Scots female writers at this time as well, Clementina Stirling Graham and Elizabeth Hamilton for instance, to add to the many men who were writing prose and verse in Scots as well as English. There were also female musicians of great ability composing airs for some of the songs being written, Isabella Scott (Mrs. Patrick Gibson) with the air to Lord Byron's 'Lochnagar' being one such.

What perhaps sets Carolina apart from this distinguished group is that she had direct access through her father and grandfather to the world of Jacobitism, and this, as was true throughout most of Perthshire up to the nineteenth century at least, allowed a view both north and south during times of great change. The Industrial Revolution was in full flow and agricultural changes were affecting all parts of Scotland. Enlightenment thought had galvanised the capital city and in general it must have seemed a time of great upheaval.

It is perhaps little wonder that the historical novels of Sir Walter Scott and the Jacobite lays of Lady Nairne should have been so well received by a public with a little time and money to spare and a need for some sort of certainty and perhaps escape as well. Carolina's songs of this genre in particular are nostalgic and view events through a somewhat rose-tinted glass but that is of course part of their charm and the reason for their popularity. It was now politically safe to be interested and show enthusiasm for these events and their participants. Indeed George IV was reported to have been particularly fond of Carolina's song 'Wha'll Be King but Chairlie', asking Nathaniel Gow the name of the air when he first heard it on his visit to Edinburgh in 1822, and on being told its title asking for it to be played again. Queen Victoria too was one of many fans of the *Lays from Strathearn** collection and appears to have owned a copy. A number of the songs in it had been popularised throughout the

*The title *Lays of Strathearn* had become *Lays from Strathearn* within ten years of the original publication in 1846.

British Isles and North America by the Scottish tenor John Wilson. He had been a pupil of the music arranger for *The Scottish Minstrel*, Finlay Dun, in Edinburgh in the 1820s, but of course he like everybody else had not been aware of the author's name.*

Another performer of the time who contributed to the popularising of Carolina's songs was the English soprano and music arranger Elizabeth Rainforth (1814-77). She lived in Edinburgh in the early 1850s and was particularly associated with 'The Hundred Pipers', which she herself published with her own arrangement in 1852. Hers too is the arrangement for 'The Auld Hoose' in *Lays from Strathearn*.

Carolina does not appear to have concerned herself with the bitter repercussions of the '45 Rising for the Highlanders and their way of life. The attempted destruction of their culture as well as the subsequent economic hardships and cruelties were perhaps not as generally known about as they are now. Perthshire was not nearly so badly affected as further north and Carolina would not have seen at first hand the results of some of the depredations that were carried out in the name of king, government or landowner. She was not a public commentator and, despite her wish to improve the national song, her songs when she wrote them were in her own view never likely to become national property. So in that sense at least she was not a spokesperson for any group or ideas. But one can be sure that had she known what we know now then it seems unlikely that her voice would have remained silent. Her deep Christian conviction and her own frugality would have been appalled at the suffering caused by greed and brutality. Her efforts and generosity to alleviate need that we know about are synonymous with her maxim that she on more than one occasion put into words: 'Religion is a walking and not a talking concern.'

*The following songs by Lady Nairne appear in John Wilson's concert lists: 'He's ower the Hills that I Lo'e weel', 'The Laird o' Cockpen', 'Charlie is My Darling', 'Land o' the Leal', 'Lass o' Gowrie', and 'Wha'll be King but Chairlie'.

THE WHITE ROSE OF GASK

Lady Nairne by Sir John Wilson Gordon, 1818.

It is perhaps surprising that Carolina did not attempt to write hymns in her later years. Her mind was dwelling increasingly on spiritual matters and her lyric ability was ideally suited to the task. The eighteenth century had proved a fertile time for hymn-writers and the great Christian revivals in America and Britain during the latter part of the nineteenth century were also to produce a large body of influential and long-lasting work. Perhaps it was the lack of suitable music to use as a springboard or the fact that hymns were not being written in great quantity during her most prolific years. Some of her lines could easily have graced devotional material. But she does not appear to have been moved very strongly in this particular direction and there is a sense that the reading of the 'Word' was more important to her than the singing of it. Perhaps she felt that song was secular and she had certainly made her name emphatically in that field.

Carolina Oliphant lived her life to the best of her not inconsiderable ability. She was a child of her time who was happy to carry out her duty as outlined to her, and she could have been much less fortunate than she was. Her family were privileged even if the star of good fortune was perhaps not shining on them quite as brightly as it had done in previous centuries. The family's adherence to the Royal House of Stuart nearly lost them everything but they were fortunate and this adherence gave the world, through Carolina's own particular gifts, some memorable songs. Her innate character, kindness and consideration helped to mould further songs, a handful of which have been described as 'immortal',* and indeed show every sign of being so.

Underpinning all her song-writing was the deep treasure trove of Scottish vernacular melody in all its particular richness, melodic and rhythmic strength and variety, and her own ability to appreciate its qualities was surely the wellspring from which much of her art stemmed. She would probably be surprised to know that folk do still sing some of her songs, and perhaps quietly irritated too that her natural reticence and humility has not prevented her name from being forever associated with our national culture. Robert Burns is the pre-eminent figure, but behind him Carolina Oliphant heads up a considerable cohort. Scots as a tongue had always been part of the national culture, but Carolina and many others as well helped

* *The Dictionary of National Biography.*

to reposition folksong and bring it from its folk tradition into an art tradition without losing its couthiness or forthright qualities. The fact that she achieved this without public knowledge or desire for recognition of that achievement is part of the charm and authenticity of her work, and her own innate skill ensured that her best songs transcend their time and continue to speak with sympathy and warmth.

The last words should be hers, for without her words the world, and Scotland in particular, would indeed be a poorer place.

> Oh! haud ye leal and true, John,
> Your day it's wearin' thro', John,
> And I'll welcome you
>   To the land o' the leal.
> Now fare ye weel, my ain John,
> This warld's cares are vain, John,
> We'll meet, and we'll be fain,
>   In the land o' the leal.

NOTES

Other Oliphants

To avoid confusion it is perhaps worth mentioning three other Oliphants who became very well-known in the nineteenth century. The closest in relationship to Lady Nairne was the musician, author and artist Thomas Oliphant (1799-1873) who was the fifth son of Ebenezer Oliphant of Condie, Perthshire. He is now probably best remembered as the author of the lyrics to the carol 'Deck the Halls with Boughs of Holly' but in his time was a leading madrigalist in London, author of many popular songs, and known as the 'Poet of the Court' as he was often commissioned to write lyrics for Royal events. His elder brother Laurence was MP for Perth between 1832 and 1837, but there is no record of either of them having met Lady Nairne.

There are two other Oliphants who also became very well-known at this time but were not closely related to the Gask family. One was the novelist Margaret Wilson Oliphant (1828-97), who wrote under the name of Mrs Oliphant and whose family originated from Kellie Castle in Fife; and the other was the extraordinary South African-born Laurence Oliphant (1829-88), author, traveller, spy, diplomat, MP, lawyer, novelist, mystic, proto-Zionist and eccentric, who traced his roots back to the Oliphants of Condie.

Other Songwriters

There are a very large number of Scottish male songwriters from the eighteenth and nineteenth centuries and indeed from earlier. Alongside the pre-eminent names of Robert Burns, Walter Scott, Robert

Tannahill, and James Hogg must be placed that of Allan Ramsay whose *Tea-table Miscellany* of 1724 was very popular and influential and would almost certainly have been known to Lady Nairne. Other names from a long list of around that time who have enriched the national song to a lesser extent would include Allan Cunningham, John Skinner, Francis Semple, Robert Crawford, James Ballantyne, Alexander Boswell, Henry Riddell, John Mayne, George Halket, John Ballantine, Thomas Davidson, John Ewen, William Glen, Hector Macneill, John Park, John Dunlop, and Thomas Lyle.

BIBLIOGRAPHY

Baptie, David, *Musical Scotland Past and Present*, J. and R. Parlane, Paisley 1894.

Barbour (Sandeman), Margaret Fraser, *Memoir of Mrs. Stewart Sandeman*, James Nisbet & Co., London, 1883.

Henderson, Rev. George, *Lady Nairne and Her Songs*, Alexander Gardner, Paisley, 1900.

Joseph Anderson (ed.), *The Oliphants in Scotland – with a selection of original documents from The Charter Chest at Gask*, printed for private circulation, 1879.

Kington-Oliphant, Thomas Laurence, *The Jacobite Lairds of Gask*, The Grampian Club, Charles Griffin & Co., London, 1870.

Maxtone-Graham, Ethel (E. Blair Oliphant), *The Oliphants of Gask – Records of a Jacobite Family*, James Nisbet and Co., London 1910.

Nairne, Caroline Baroness, *Lays from Strathearn*, Addison & Co., London, and Paterson & Co., Edinburgh and Glasgow, 1850.

Nairne, Caroline Baroness, *Lays of Strathearn*, Paterson & Co., Edinburgh & Glasgow, 1846.

Private papers of Carolina Oliphant.

Private papers of Dr Alexander Stewart, Bonskeid.

Private papers of May Stewart (Oliphant), Bonskeid.

Purdie, Robert (ed.), *The Scottish Minstrel*, Vols. 1-6, Edinburgh, 1821-24.

Redpath, Jean, *'Will ye no' come back again' – The Songs of Lady Nairne*, CD Release, Greentrax recordings, Cockenzie, 2008.

Rogers, Rev. Charles (ed.), *Life and Songs of the Baroness Nairne, with a memoir and poems of Caroline Oliphant the younger*, Charles Griffin & Co., London, 1869.

Rogers, Rev. Charles (ed.), *The Modern Scottish Minstrel*, 6 Vols., Adam & Charles Black, Edinburgh, 1855-60.

Simpson, Margaret Stewart Barbour, *The Scottish Songstress – Caroline Baroness Nairne*, Oliphant, Anderson & Ferrier, Edinburgh & London, 1894.

The Miniature Series – The Songs of Lady Nairne, Nimmo Hay and Mitchell, Edinburgh 1910.

The Songs of Lady Nairne, T.N. Foulis, London & Edinburgh, 1911.

THE SONGS OF LADY NAIRNE

This list contains all songs previously included in published collections of Lady Nairne's works. It is not certain, however, that all of them are her own work. She was in the habit of entering into her notebooks anything that pleased her, sometimes with the intention of alteration at some point but clearly sometimes just to have a record of something she enjoyed and might wish to refer to in the future. To begin with after her death her wish for anonymity during her lifetime made it difficult for publishers, and there was a tendency to publish and attribute to her anything that was found in her notebooks and written in her own hand or even in another hand. If there is any doubt as to provenance, then wherever possible information of sources or author alongside the relevant title is provided. Of the 103 songs listed here, approximately 25 are reworkings of older songs and at least four are unlikely to be by Lady Nairne at all.

Adieu to Strathearn

A Heavenly Muse

Ah, Little Did My Mother Think

Aikin Drum

Archie's an Archer

Attainted Scottish Nobles, The

Auld Hoose, The

Auld Langsyne
   (The oldest known version of this song was titled 'Old Long Syne' and composed by Sir Robert Aytoun, 1570-1638.)

Ayrshire Lassie, The

Banks of the Earn, The

Bannocks o' Barley Meal
   (Original attributed to William, 2nd Marquess of Lothian (1661-1722) and titled 'Cakes o' Crowdy'.)

Bess Is Young, and Bess Is Fair

Boat Song o' Forth, The

Boat Song o' the Clyde, The
  (The apparent allusion in
  this song to Queen Vic-
  toria's visit to the Clyde
  is a puzzle. The visit took
  place in the late summer of
  1847, two years after Lady
  Nairne's death. Nor do the
  verses bear any of Lady
  Nairne's stamp. It is highly
  probable that this is not
  her work. It first appeared
  in the second edition of
  Lays of Strathearn.)
Bonnie Ran the Burnie doun
Bonniest Lass in a' the Warld,
  The
Bonny Gascon Ha'

Cairney Burn
Caller Herrin'
Castell Gloom
Cauld Kail in Aberdeen
Charlie Is My Darling
Charlie's Landing
Chief Thy Name Doth Linger
  ever
Convict's Farewell, The
County Meeting, The
Cradle Song

Dead Who Have Died in The
  Lord, The
  (It seems likely that this
  was composed by James
  Glassford, a legal writer

and poet who was an Edin-
  burgh contemporary of the
  Nairnes.)
Doun the Burn, Davie
  (Original by Robert
  Crawford)
Duncan Gray
Dunnottar Castle

Eppie Macnab

Fareweel, Edinburgh
Fareweel, O Fareweel
Fell He on the Field of Fame?
Fife Laird, The

Gathering Song
Gie's a Blast, King Jamie
Gude Nicht, and Joy Be wi' Ye
  A'
  (All versions of this song
  were based on the Border
  ballad, 'Armstrong's Good-
  night', which is attributed
  to one of the Border clan
  of Armstrongs for his part
  in the assassination of Sir
  John Carmichael, Scottish
  Warden of the Middle
  Marches, in 1600.)

Happy Land
  (This is based on the hymn
  'There Is a Happy Land' by
  the Scottish schoolmaster,
  Andrew Young (1807-89).

It was first published in
1838.)
Heiress, The
Here's to Them That Are Gane
Her Home She Is Leaving
He's Lifeless amang the Rude
   Billows
He's ower the Hills That I Lo'e
   weel
Hey the Rantin' Murray's Ha'
Hundred Pipers, The
Huntingtower

Idle Laddie, The

Jamie the Laird
Jeanie Deans
John Tod
Joy of My Earliest Days

Kind Robin Lo'es Me
Kitty Reid's House

Lady Grange, The
Laird o' Cockpen, The
Lament of the Covenanter's
   Widow
Land o' the Leal, The
Lass o' Gowrie, The
Lass of Livingstane, The
Lay by Yere Bawbee

Maiden's Vow, The
Mitherless Lammie, The
My Ain Kind Dearie O
My Bonnie Hieland Laddie

O never, O never Thou'lt Meet
   Me again
Oh! Ocean Blue
   (This song was taken from
   Lady Nairne's notebooks
   but was not in her hand-
   writing.)
O Mountains Wild
O Stately Stood the Baron's Ha'
O weel's Me on My Ain Man
O Wha Is This Comin'?

Pentland Hills, The
Pleughman, The

Regalia, The
Rest Is not here
Robin's Nest, The
Rowan Tree, The

Saw Ye nae My Peggy
Saw Ye ne'er a Lonely Lassie
Songs of My Native Land
St Andrews Toun

Tammy
There Grows a Bonnie Brier
   Bush
To Thee, Lov'd Dee
True Love Is Watered aye with
   Tears
Trump of War, The

Voice of Spring, The

Wake, Irishmen, Wake

We'll Gang na mair a' Rovin'
    (Chorus from 'The Jolly
    Beggar' attributed to James
    V.)
We're A' Noddin'
We're A' Singin'
Wha'll Be King but Charlie?
What Do Ye Think o' Geordie
    noo?
When first I Got Married

White Rose of June, The
Widow Are Ye Waukin'?
Will Ye no' Come back again
Women Are A' Gane Wud, The
Would You Be Young Again

Ye'll Mount, Gudeman
Ye Spires of Banff
Youths' Soiree

PICTURE CREDITS

p. 6: William III and Mary II. Granger Historical Picture Archive/ Alamy Stock Photo.

p. 8: James Francis Edward Stuart. Ian Dagnall/Alamy Stock Photo.

p. 10: Laurence Oliphant, 6th Laird. Historic Images/Alamy Stock Photo.

p. 12: Charles Edward Stuart. Ian Dagnall/Alamy Stock Photo.

p. 24: Laurence Oliphant, 7th Laird. Historic Images/Alamy Stock Photo.

p. 50: Niel Gow. National Galleries of Scotland/Alamy Stock Photo.

p. 70: Charles Edward Stuart. Alamy Stock Photo.

p. 95: The new house of Gask. Falkensteinfoto/Alamy Stock Photo.

p. 128: Lady Nairne and her son William. National Galleries of Scotland. Bequeathed by K. Oliphant 1903.

p. 169: Lady Nairne. The Picture Art Collection/Alamy Stock Photo.